Truth Shall Triumph

A Study of Pentecostal Doctrines

RALPH VINCENT REYNOLDS

Truth Shall Triumph

A Study of Pentecostal Doctrines

Truth Shall Triumph

by Ralph Vincent Reynolds

Hazelwood, MO 63042-2299

Printing History: 1968, 1975, 1976, 1977, 1978, 1980, 1981, 1983, 1984, 1986, 1987, 1988, 1990, 1991, 1993, 1995, 1996
Revised: 1998, 2000, 2002

ISBN 0-912315-07-5

Cover Design by Paul Povolni

Printed in United States of America

Printed by

WORD AFLAME® PRESS
8855 DUNN ROAD
HAZELWOOD, MO 63042-2299

Contents

Preface

In writing this book, I have been very much aware that I was writing for teachers. My desire was that this book should not be only a textbook on doctrine, but also a book stating Bible truths in a manner that will assist teachers to impart these truths to their classes.

Having this purpose in mind, I divided each chapter into six sections, each of which deals with a Bible truth. In dealing with the thought of each section, the following steps are taken:

1. *Statement of Scripture.* Always the proper place to begin is with the Word of God. We should always state the Scripture and then the truth that the Scripture teaches. Generally two or three verses of Scripture are stated. (See Matthew 18:16.)

2. *Statement of truth.* This is the proposition that is stated in the Scripture. Many make the mistake of stating a proposition and then going to the Scripture to prove it. This, of course, is wrong; the correct thing to do is always to go to the Scripture first to learn what the Scripture says, and then to write the proposition.

3. *Exposition of truth.* Under this heading is the argument to prove the proposition, the exegesis of Scripture, and the definition and explanation of terms.

4. *Application of truth.* Every truth should have an application in the life and experience of the individual. As truth is taught, the teacher should apply this truth to the hearts of the students in the class.

Each teacher must decide to what extent these Bible truths may be developed and taught on the level of the class he teaches. Having this in mind, I have striven for simplicity, clarity, and logic. I have attempted to state these Bible truths sufficiently clear and simple that primary teachers may be able to decide what to teach their children and to teach it with such simplicity and clarity that the children will be indoctrinated with basic and fundamental Bible truth. At the same time, I have attempted to develop the lessons sufficiently that adult teachers may have a foundation to advance forward into more profound studies of doctrine and theology.

Let us always remember that if we have not imparted truth to others we have taught nothing. As teachers, it is not our purpose to impress others with a display of our knowledge, but rather to impart that knowledge to others. We might better teach one simple truth well than to confuse our class with a scholarly presentation of deep truths beyond their comprehension and, as a result, teach nothing. For this reason, let us keep to the level of our class and make a logical presentation of Scripture, one truth at a time.

To the instruction of boys and girls in our Sunday schools with Bible truth, this book is dedicated.

Chapter 1
The Infallible Word

I. THE BIBLE IS THE WORD OF GOD

A. STATEMENT OF SCRIPTURE

1. "Thy Word is truth" (John 17:17).

2. "All scripture is given by inspiration of God" (II Timothy 3:16).

3. "For the prophecy came not in old time by the will of man: but holy men of God spake as they were moved by the Holy Ghost" (II Peter 1:21).

B. STATEMENT OF TRUTH

The Bible is the Word of God. God is the author of the Bible.

The Bible is God's message to man.

C. EXPOSITION OF TRUTH

1. *The meaning of "Bible."* The word "Bible" is derived from the Greek *biblia* and means "the books." Ancient books were written by hand as scrolls upon the biblus, or papyrus reed, and from this custom came the Greek word that was finally applied to the sacred books.

However, we should not think of the Bible as being plural, for it is one complete whole. The Bible is not only "the books" but it is "the Book" (Hebrews 10:7). It is the Book that stands as high above all other books as the heaven is high above the earth.

2. *What the Bible contains.* The Bible contains sixty-six books divided into the Old and New Testaments. The word "testament" means "covenant," and is a term by which God designates the relation between Himself and His people.

a. Old Testament (thirty-nine books). The Old Testament deals with man's beginning, his knowledge of sin, and his need of salvation. It also gives the calling and history of the Jewish nation.

b. New Testament (twenty-seven books). The New Testament gives the history and application of the redemption wrought by the Lord Jesus Christ.

3. *God used human instrumentality.* In writing the Bible, God used possibly forty men over a period of about 1,600 years, beginning about 1,500 B.C., when Moses began to write the Pentateuch, to about A.D. 97, when the apostle John finished his writings.

Throughout the Bible God used humans to do the writing. In Scripture, only three times did God Himself write, as follows:

a. God wrote the Ten Commandments upon tables of stone (Exodus 31:18).

b. God wrote with a finger upon Belshazzar's wall (Daniel 5:5).

c. Jesus wrote upon the ground in the Temple area (John 8:6, 8).

The first, the giving of the law, was broken by man; the last, an act of grace, was trampled under foot by man.

4. *How God wrote the Bible.* God wrote through people whom He had chosen, by a process known as inspiration. All Scripture was given by inspiration of God (II Timothy 3:16). The phrase "given by inspiration of God" comes from one Greek word meaning "God-breathed." It actually means that God breathed out through these men, or literally, these men became God's vocal chords. Inspiration is the strong, con-

scious breathing of God into people, qualifying them to give utterance to truth. Inspiration is God speaking through humans, and the Bible is, therefore, just as much the Word of God as though God spoke every single word of it with His own lips. The Scriptures are the result of divine breathing out, just as human speech is uttered by the breath of a person's mouth.

D. APPLICATION OF TRUTH

Since God is the author of the Bible, it is God's message to humanity. As such, it is the highest authority that humans have to govern themselves in matters of faith and practice. There is no higher authority for humanity than God's Word. What more definite authority could humans desire than what is invested in the Word of their Creator? It is not the authority of the church to decide what the Scriptures teach, but rather it is the authority of the Scriptures to decide what the church should teach.

E. DEFINITION OF TERMS

1. *Scriptures*: This word is derived from the Latin and means "the writings."

2. *Papyrus*: A reed or bulrush, and the ancient writing material made from it.

3. *Pentateuch*: The first five books of the Old Testament.

II. THE BIBLE IS FULLY INSPIRED

A. STATEMENT OF SCRIPTURE

1. "Till heaven and earth pass, one jot or one tittle shall in no wise pass from the law, till all be fulfilled" (Matthew 5:18).

2. "All Scripture is given by inspiration of God" (II Timothy 3:16).

3. "If any man shall take away from the words of the book of this prophecy, God shall take away his part out of

the book of life" (Revelation 22:19).

B. STATEMENT OF TRUTH

The plenary inspiration of the Scriptures is a fact. The Bible is fully inspired. It does not just contain the Word of God; the Bible is the Word of God.

C. EXPOSITION OF TRUTH

Throughout the years the inspiration of the Bible has been attacked by its enemies, and in modern times it has become fashionable in some church circles to question the full inspiration of the Scriptures. These false friends within the nominal, professing church are its greatest foes and do the greatest damage to the truth discussed here.

Two false views concerning inspiration are:

1. At certain times and under certain circumstances God may speak to humans through certain parts of the Bible; that is, parts of the Bible may become the Word of God under certain conditions and circumstances.

2. The Bible is not in itself the Word of God but contains the Word of God. This false concept permits the idea that part of the Bible is true but the rest is error and that truth is brought to us in a collection of legends and myths.

The fallacy of the foregoing views is so apparent that it seems folly even to waste words in refuting them. How can truth be enclosed in a shell of falsehood? How can God, who cannot lie (Hebrews 6:18), speak truth to humanity in lies? If part of the Bible is false, who is the judge to discern truth from error? The only possible conclusion is that the plenary inspiration of the Bible is a fact.

A few of the reasons why the Bible is fully inspired are:

1. Jesus gave the Old Testament His full sanction (Matthew 5:18).

2. It is the product of one mastermind. Although God used forty men over a period of sixteen hundred years, the unity of the Bible proves it has one divine author.

3. The types, symbols, and ceremonies of the Old Testament are all fulfilled and revealed in the New Testament.

4. The prophecies prove it to be God's Word. Bible prophecies have been fulfilled in the past and are being fulfilled in the present.

5. The Bible reveals man to himself. This proves that the Creator of humanity must be the author of the Bible.

6. The Bible always lifts humanity and brings good. The fruits that follow it prove it to be God's Word.

7. The world has recognized it as being God's Word. Whole libraries have been written to interpret it, and before it sages bow.

D. APPLICATION OF TRUTH

In all matters pertaining to faith and moral conduct, we must turn to the Bible, for here we find God's message for us. We must accept, believe, and obey all of God's Word. It is not our prerogative to accept part of the Word and reject the rest. We should never attempt to be a critic of the Bible—instead, it is our critic and judge.

E. DEFINITION OF TERMS

1. *Jot and tittle*: These are small letters in the Hebrew alphabet. In English, an equivalent phrase is "the dotting of an 'i' and the crossing of a 't.'"

2. *Plenary*: Full, complete, absolute.

III. THE BIBLE IS VERBALLY INSPIRED

A. STATEMENT OF SCRIPTURE

1. "All Scripture is given by inspiration of God" (II Timothy 3:16).

2. "Of which salvation the prophets have enquired and searched diligently, who prophesied of the grace that should come unto you" (I Peter 1:10).

B. STATEMENT OF TRUTH

The Bible is verbally inspired in the original Hebrew and Greek in which it was written. That is, each word accurately communicates God's message.

C. EXPOSITION OF TRUTH

It is impossible for God to make a mistake. It is also impossible for God to lie. Therefore, because the Bible is the Word of God and fully inspired, it must also be verbally inspired. There can be no errors in it. As God breathed through people to write His Word, they wrote it word by word and letter by letter as God desired it. Errors could be made by translators, and there may be errors in modern translations and versions, but there could be no error in the original Hebrew of the Old Testament and the original Greek of the New Testament.

A few of the reasons why the Bible is verbally inspired are:

1. The writers themselves say so.

Moses: "These are the words which the LORD hath commanded" (Exodus 35:1).

Jeremiah: "And the LORD said unto me, Behold, I have put my words in thy mouth" (Jeremiah 1:9).

Ezekiel: "The word of the LORD came expressly unto Ezekiel" (Ezekiel 1:3).

Amos: "The words of Amos . . . which he saw concerning Israel" (Amos 1:1).

John: "The revelation of Jesus Christ, which God gave unto him" (Revelation 1:1).

2. The writers often did not fully understand what they wrote. God gave the words but not necessarily the fullness of the divine purpose. The prophets did not minister

to themselves but to us and inquired into what they wrote (I Peter 1:10-12). Daniel did not understand all that he wrote (Daniel 12:8-9). Certainly David did not understand the prophetic fulfillment of the parting of the garments and the piercing of the hands and feet (Psalm 22:16-18).

3. The Bible places importance upon simple words: "Yet once more" (Hebrews 12:27).

4. The Bible places importance upon the tense of a verb: "I am" (Matthew 22:32).

5. The Bible places importance upon the singular versus plural form of a word, merely one letter, *s*, in English: "seed," not "seeds" (Galatians 3:16).

6. The testimony of Christ proves that the Bible was verbally inspired: "jot or tittle" (Matthew 5:18).

7. If the Bible contained the slightest error, no matter how small, then it could contain greater errors. It must be verbally inspired to be the Word of God.

D. APPLICATION OF TRUTH

We should strive to understand the Word of God as written in the original texts and study it carefully, even to each word and letter.

E. DEFINITION OF TERM

Verbal inspiration: Each word is inspired. Not only does the message come from God, but also each word is given by God.

IV. THE BIBLE IS COMPLETE, LACKING NOTHING

A. STATEMENT OF SCRIPTURE

1. "Ye shall not add unto the word which I command you, neither shall ye diminish ought from it" (Deuteronomy 4:2).

2. "Add thou not unto his words, lest he reprove thee, and thou be found a liar" (Proverbs 30:6).

3. "If any man shall add unto these things, God shall add unto him the plagues that are written in this book" (Revelation 22:18).

B. STATEMENT OF TRUTH

The Bible is complete. Nothing needs to be added to the Word of God to make it God's complete message to humanity.

C. EXPOSITION OF TRUTH

1. *Warnings against adding to the Bible.* There are three solemn warnings in the Bible against adding to the Word of God. These alone prove that the Bible is complete and is God's whole message to humanity, needing nothing to be added.

2. *The Apocrypha is not part of the Bible.* The Apocrypha is not acknowledged by Jews or the Protestant Christian church as being inspired. The Apocrypha contains a great deal of legendary nonsense and some gross historical errors. There is no reference to the Apocrypha in the New Testament. It should never be considered as part of God's Word.

D. APPLICATION OF TRUTH

All teaching and preaching of spiritual truths must come from the Bible. Any teaching that we cannot find in the Bible we must reject as not being divinely inspired. If it cannot be found in God's Word, then it is only of human origin. If anyone claims to speak the Word of God but what he says does not harmonize with the Bible, then he is a false prophet and is in danger of judgment, for he is adding to God's Word.

E. DEFINITION OF TERM

Apocrypha: Fourteen books or additions to books included in the Roman Catholic Old Testament but not in the Jewish Scriptures or the Protestant Bible.

V. THE BIBLE NEVER CONTRADICTS ITSELF

A. STATEMENT OF SCRIPTURE

1. "The book of the generation of Jesus Christ" (Matthew 1:1). "And Jesus himself began to be . . ." (Luke 3:23).

2. "And seeing the multitudes, he went up into a mountain" (Matthew 5:1). "And he came down with them, and stood in the plain" (Luke 6:17).

3. "And those that died in the plague were twenty and four thousand" (Numbers 25:9). "Neither let us commit fornication, as some of them committed, and fell in one day three and twenty thousand" (I Corinthians 10:8).

4. "Baptizing them in the name of the Father, and of the Son, and of the Holy Ghost" (Matthew 28:19). "Repent, and be baptized every one of you in the name of Jesus Christ for the remission of sins" (Acts 2:38).

B. STATEMENT OF TRUTH

There are in the Bible certain supposed mistakes and contradictions, but when properly understood these supposed contradictions all disappear.

C. EXPOSITION OF TRUTH

The Bible, if correctly interpreted, never contradicts itself. The so-called mistakes and contradictions only reveal human lack of understanding of the Bible. When God's Word is properly understood, all such apparent errors disappear. This is another proof of the infallibility of the Bible.

In this lesson we give four examples of supposed contradictions, with the explanation for each. What is true of these four examples is also true of all other supposed mistakes.

1. *Genealogies of our Lord.* Matthew's Gospel traces the genealogy of our Lord on Joseph's side back to Abraham, to show Christ as the legal heir to the throne of Israel. Luke's Gospel traces the genealogy on Mary's side back to Adam, to emphasize Christ's true humanity and to show Him as the promised seed of the woman.

2. *The Sermon on the Mount.* There were two sermons: one was preached to the disciples on the mountain; the other was preached to the crowd on the plain. Apparently Jesus preached the sermon on the mountain and then came down to the plain and repeated the sermon to the crowd.

3. *Paul's supposed mistake.* In the Book of Numbers we read of the total number who died, while Paul stated how many died in one day.

4. *The baptismal formula.* There is no contradiction here. Jesus did not tell His disciples to baptize using the words "Father, Son, and Holy Ghost." He told them to baptize in "the name" of the Father, Son, and Holy Ghost. The words "Father, Son and Holy Ghost" are not names but titles pointing to one person who has one name. That name is Jesus.

D. APPLICATION OF TRUTH

We should study the Bible carefully to understand its exact meaning. If there is any apparent mistake or contradiction, it is evident that we do not understand clearly. We should recognize at all times that the Bible is absolutely accurate and infallible. We should never change, in the slightest manner, the Word of God but rather seek the Holy Ghost to illuminate our minds with a clear knowledge of the Scriptures.

E. DEFINITION OF TERMS

1. *Genealogy:* A record of family ancestors traced back from generation to generation.

2. *Baptismal formula*: The set form of words spoken by the minister as he baptizes an individual.

VI. A KNOWLEDGE OF GOD'S WORD COMES THROUGH CERTAIN METHODS ORDAINED BY GOD

A. STATEMENT OF SCRIPTURE

1. "Knowing this first, that no prophecy of the scripture is of any private interpretation" (II Peter 1:20).

2. "When he, the Spirit of truth, is come, he will guide you into all truth" (John 16:13).

3. "And God hath set some in the church, first apostles, secondarily prophets, thirdly teachers" (I Corinthians 12:28).

B. STATEMENT OF TRUTH

There are certain means and methods that God has ordained to bring an understanding of His Word to humanity. Some of these methods are:

1. Hearing the Word preached, taught and expounded by Holy Ghost–filled people.
2. A careful reading and study of the Word.
3. A divine illumination of the Word by the Holy Spirit.

C. EXPOSITION OF TRUTH

Some people have claimed that they needed no one to teach them because the Holy Ghost was their teacher. It is true that the Holy Spirit is the best teacher, but the attitude that no one can teach us is a dangerous one that may lead to spiritual pride and many errors. The teaching ministry is very important in the church. Jesus has placed teachers in the body (I Corinthians 12:28; Ephesians 4:11). Jesus instructed His disciples to go and teach all nations (Matthew 28:19-20).

God has definitely ordained that the truth of His Word

should be imparted to others through the ministry of teaching. If a person is not willing to be taught by a Holy Ghost–filled teacher, it is doubtful whether the Holy Spirit can teach him. Moreover, a person who is unwilling to be taught disqualifies himself from being a teacher or minister to others.

It is true that the best teacher is the Holy Ghost (John 16:13). We learn divine truth by divine illumination. It takes the author of the Bible Himself to make clear and plain the profound and eternal truths of the Bible. For this reason teachers of God's Word should be Spirit-filled and should continually look to the Holy Spirit to anoint their ministry. Likewise, students of God's Word should continually look to the Holy Spirit to open their minds and hearts to comprehend divine truth through divine illumination.

There are three things that the student of the Bible should maintain:

1. A heart that hungers after truth for the sake of truth alone.

2. A heart that is teachable and willing to be taught.

3. A heart that will apply itself to the reading and study of God's Word (I Timothy 4:13; II Timothy 2:15).

There are a few simple principles for understanding the Bible that we should always remember:

1. Symbolic language will need explaining, such as the parables of our Lord and certain symbols in Revelation, but on the whole we are to interpret the Bible literally. For example, the Book of Acts and the Epistles use plain, literal language that we should understand accordingly.

2. The New Testament is divided into four main divisions:

a. The Gospels—what Jesus did to provide salvation.

b. The Acts of the Apostles—the history of the early church and the plan of salvation.

c. The Epistles—letters to the churches stating how

we continue in our salvation and live the Christian life.

d. Revelation—the future of the church and the end of this age.

3. The Bible always exalts Jesus Christ. Any teaching that degrades Jesus is erroneous.

4. The Bible is always in harmony with itself. We should not try to establish doctrine on one isolated passage of Scripture, unless we can demonstrate that this doctrine is in harmony with the entire Bible.

5. Truth is always well-balanced, sound, and solidly built upon the Word.

D. APPLICATION OF TRUTH

We should recognize all the methods God has ordained to impart a knowledge of His Word to our hearts, apply ourselves to the study of the Bible, be faithful in our attendance to all Bible classes taught by our pastors in the church, and maintain a heart that hungers after truth.

E. DEFINITION OF TERMS

1. *Revelation*: The act of God by which He communicates to the human mind previously unknown knowledge of Himself and His Word.

2. *Illumination*: The influence of the Spirit upon the minds of people so that they will understand spiritual things and specifically the Word of God.

QUESTIONS

1. Approximately how many people did God use in writing the Bible?

2. On what three occasions did God Himself write without using a human agency?

3. Explain clearly the expression "given by inspiration of God."

4. What are two false views of inspiration that are popular in the nominal church today?

5. Show clearly the fallacy of the errors referred to in the preceding question.

6. What is the meaning of the term "verbal inspiration"?

7. Give an example where the Bible places importance upon (a) the tense of a verb and (b) a mere letter.

8. What three warnings are given against adding to the Bible?

9. Why is the Apocrypha not part of the Bible?

10. State five principles to remember in understanding the Bible.

PROJECTS

1. Memorize in order the names of the sixty-six books of the Bible.

2. Through research, find the necessary information and write a brief history of the work of either John Wycliffe or William Tyndale.

NOTES

Chapter 2

Humans Are Sinners

I. HUMANS WERE CREATED IN THE IMAGE OF GOD

A. STATEMENT OF SCRIPTURE

1. "So God created man in His own image, in the image of God created He him; male and female created He them" (Genesis 1:27).

2. "For in the image of God made He man" (Genesis 9:6).

3. "Forasmuch as he is the image and glory of God . . ." (I Corinthians 11:7).

B. STATEMENT OF TRUTH

God created humans in His own image. Since humans were made in God's own image and likeness, they are God's highest act of creation.

C. EXPOSITION OF TRUTH

1. *Humans are created beings.* Humans have not evolved from some lower order of life. The theory of evolution advanced by modern science is wild imagination that cannot possibly be proved. There is abundant evidence that humanity has degenerated rather than advanced. There has been no proof that humans developed from the body of some brute beast. It is true that

knowledge is increasing, but human intellectual powers and capabilities have not increased.

Humans were created by a definite act of their Creator. Only of humans is it said that God created them in His own image, that God breathed into them the breath of life, and that they became living souls (Genesis 1:27; 2:7). As such, humanity is the crowning work of God, and never will there be on earth a higher order of beings than humans.

2. *Humans were created in God's own image.*

a. The moral nature of humans. Possibly the greatest way in which humans resemble their Maker is in their moral nature. God created Adam and Eve as sinless with an absolute purity and innocence. In fact, they were clothed with the righteousness of God. Because of this, they were able to have fellowship with God. This righteousness they lost in the Fall, which caused them to realize that they were naked.

b. The intellectual nature of humans. God gave Adam the intelligence necessary to name all living creatures and have dominion over the earth. He gave humans the power to reason and to make decisions. He created them as free moral agents.

c. The physical appearance of humans. God is Spirit and invisible, but it was in the plan and purpose of Deity to manifest Himself in flesh. If the image of God has any reference to physical appearance, it could only be to the likeness of the man Christ Jesus, who was to be born at Bethlehem. So far as time is concerned, the advent of Christ took place at a definite point of history, but so far as God is concerned, who dwells in eternity, He planned it and saw it from the beginning.

d. The unlimited potential of humans. God gave humans unlimited potential. They can rise higher and sink lower than any other of God's creatures. There seems to be no bottom to the depths into which men or women can fall. Likewise, they have the capacity of yielding to God and becoming a vessel filled with His Spirit. There seems to be no limit to the heights to which God can lift them.

D. APPLICATION OF TRUTH

The knowledge that we were made in the image of God should inspire us to rise to sublime heights in Christ and permit His beauty and nature to be seen in us. We should recognize the theory of evolution as erroneous and inadequate to explain our existence and nature.

E. DEFINITION OF TERM

Evolution: A false scientific theory that humans gradually developed from a lower order of animal life.

II. HUMANS WERE CREATED RIGHTEOUS AND WITHOUT SIN

A. STATEMENT OF SCRIPTURE

1. "But of the tree of the knowledge of good and evil, thou shalt not eat of it" (Genesis 2:17).

2. "Wherefore, as by one man sin entered into the world, and death by sin . . ." (Romans 5:12).

3. "And that ye put on the new man, which after God is created in righteousness and true holiness" (Ephesians 4:24).

B. STATEMENT OF TRUTH

Adam and Eve were created innocent and without the knowledge of sin.

C. EXPOSITION OF TRUTH

It is quite clear that Adam and Eve were created innocent and without the knowledge of sin, for the following reasons:

1. They were created in the image of God, which would, of necessity, be without sin.

2. They did not have the knowledge of good and evil (Genesis 2:17).

3. Sin entered the world through their act of disobedience.

4. The new man is created in righteousness and true holiness.

It was this innocence of Adam and Eve that enabled them to have fellowship with their Creator. God is absolutely pure and holy and can never have fellowship sin. Humans had to be absolutely sinless in order for God to walk with them. Actually it would seem that Adam and Eve were clothed with the righteousness of God. It was this clothing of righteousness that they lost in the Fall and that caused them to realize they were naked.

D. APPLICATION OF TRUTH

There can be no true fellowship with God without righteousness.

In order to have fellowship with God, humans must be born again, created again in righteousness and true holiness. If they lose this, they lose communion with God.

III. HUMANS FELL THROUGH AN ACT OF DISOBEDIENCE

A. STATEMENT OF SCRIPTURE

1. "And when the woman saw that the tree was good for food, and that it was pleasant to the eyes, and a tree to be desired to make one wise, she took of the fruit thereof, and did eat, and gave also unto her husband with her; and he did eat" (Genesis 3:6).

2. "For as by one man's disobedience many were made sinners, so by the obedience of one shall many be made righteous" (Romans 5:19).

B. STATEMENT OF TRUTH

It was through a single act of disobedience that our first parents fell and sin entered the human family.

C. EXPOSITION OF TRUTH

That sin is a definite act of disobedience to the revealed will of God is proven clearly and conclusively in the fall of our first parents.

1. *Temptation is not sin.* This is clearly shown in that our Lord was tempted in all points like as we are, yet without sin (Hebrews 4:15). It is possible to be fiercely tempted and yet not to sin, by refusing to yield. It is the yielding to temptation that brings sin. Therefore, sin is a definite act of yielding to temptation. Adam and Eve did not have to disobey; they could have resisted and remained sinless. "Blessed is the man that endureth temptation" (James 1:12).

2. *There are definite steps that precede the act of sin.* The act of sin follows temptation and generally follows certain steps. James mentioned this progression in his epistle (James 1:14-15), stating four steps: (a) a person is drawn away with lust; (b) the person is enticed; (c) lust is conceived; (d) sin occurs. We see these steps in the temptation of Eve (Genesis 3:6): (a) she saw; (b) she desired; (c) she took; (d) she ate. Again there are definite steps in the sin of Achan (Joshua 7:21): (a) he saw; (b) he coveted; (c) he took; (d) he hid. Clearly, there are steps leading up to an act of sin. There is generally plenty of warning, and the guilty one is inexcusable.

We may study the steps leading to Eve's act of disobedience from another angle:

a. Unbelief: The first thing Satan succeeded in doing was to plant the seed of unbelief in Eve's heart. "Yea, hath God said . . . ?" (Genesis 3:1).

b. Changing God's Word: Eve both changed and added to God's Word. God said nothing about touching the fruit, and death was certain rather than just a possibility. "Neither shall ye touch it, lest ye die" (Genesis 3:3).

c. Disobedience: The act of sin followed unbelief and the changing of God's Word. The greatest factor in successfully conquering temptation is maintaining a strong and unshaken faith in the Word of God.

3. *Eve's temptation compared with Christ's temptation.* In both instances we may sum up the temptation under "all that is in the world, the lust of the flesh, and the lust of the eyes, and the pride of life" (I John 2:16).

Eve's temptation (Genesis 3:6): good for food; pleasant to the eyes; desired to make wise.

Christ's temptation (Luke 4:3-10): turn stone to bread; possess the kingdoms of this world; cause the angels to perform a spectacular rescue.

Although there is a similarity in the two temptations, there is a vast difference in the results. Eve doubted the Word of God and yielded to sin; Christ resisted temptation by the power of the Word.

4. *Adam's responsibility.* God created humans as free moral agents with the power of decision and the responsibility of choice. God desired the fellowship of His image creature, but that fellowship had to be freely given. There is no such thing as true fellowship if it occurs through compulsion. Fellowship must be freely given. Therefore, God gave humans the responsibility of choice, and Adam's act of disobedience was his own responsibility.

Adam's act of disobedience challenged the sovereignty of God! He deliberately chose the fellowship of Eve over that of God and broke fellowship with his Creator. All this Adam did in his willful act of disobedience.

D. APPLICATION OF TRUTH

No Christian need yield to temptation. It is possible for everyone to follow the example of Christ and be victorious over Satan. We may do so by standing upon the power of God's Word. There are generally warnings as sin progresses through definite steps, which leave a person without excuse when he commits an act of sin.

IV. HUMANITY DIED BECAUSE OF DISOBEDIENCE

A. STATEMENT OF SCRIPTURE

1. "For dust thou art, and unto dust shalt thou return" (Genesis 3:19).

2. "Wherefore, as by one man sin entered into the world, and death by sin . . ." (Romans 5:12).

3. "For the wages of sin is death" (Romans 6:23).

4. "And sin, when it is finished, bringeth forth death" (James 1:15).

B. STATEMENT OF TRUTH

The result of sin is always death. "The soul that sinneth, it shall die" (Ezekiel 18:4) is one of God's eternal laws. It was true in the experience of Adam and has been true ever since. There is no escaping the truth that death is always the result of sin.

C. EXPOSITION OF TRUTH

God is sovereign and the Creator. As such He has the right to direct the lives of His creatures, to lay down laws that will govern them. Any act of disobedience is a direct challenge to His sovereignty. When an individual disobeys God, he does not recognize God as sovereign and asserts that God no longer has any right to direct his life. In effect, he places self on the level of deity. But there can only be one God. Sin challenges the very being of deity, and God's honor demands that all sin be punished with death.

God created the universe to operate by definite, God-ordained laws. When people break these laws, destruction and chaos follow. Just as physical life demands oxygen, even so spiritual and eternal life demands a constant flow of fellowship and communion with God. Just as suffocation shuts off the breath and the supply of oxygen, bringing physical death, even so when the Spirit of God is shut off from people, they die spiritually, which in turn results in eternal death. This is exactly what Adam did when he broke fellowship with God in order to maintain fellowship with Eve. God's absolute holiness can never have fellowship with sin. Therefore when Adam sinned, he broke fellowship with His Creator and death had to be the result.

We see from this exposition that there were at least two reasons (either one of which would have been sufficient) why Adam died because of his act of disobedience.

Adam immediately died spiritually, and physical death instantly began to work in his body, which resulted in death 930 years later.

D. APPLICATION OF TRUTH

After six thousand years the laws of God still hold true. Anyone who disobeys the will of God and commits an act of sin shall die. However, Jesus Christ has provided a means of salvation. Even as disobedience brings death, obedience to the gospel brings life eternal.

E. DEFINITION OF TERMS

1. *Physical death:* The separation of the spirit and soul from the body, which results in the corruption of the material frame.

2. *Spiritual death:* The separation of the human spirit from God, or alienation from the life of God.

3. *Eternal death:* Spiritual death continued after physical death, a state of eternal separation from God in conscious torment.

V. NATURE AND ALL HUMANITY WERE AFFECTED BY THE FALL

A. STATEMENT OF SCRIPTURE

1. "And the LORD God said unto the serpent. . . . And to Adam he said, Unto dust shalt thou return" (Genesis 3:14-19).

2. "All have sinned, and come short of the glory of God" (Romans 3:23).

3. "For as in Adam all die . . ." (I Corinthians 15:22).

B. STATEMENT OF TRUTH

All nature was affected and was cursed by God because of the fall of humanity; the entire human race fell with Adam, for all were in his loins.

C. EXPOSITION OF TRUTH

1. *The ground was cursed.* God cursed the ground so that it would not only yield what is good but it also would bring forth thorns and thistles. God had created humans out of the dust of the ground, and now that they would die they would return to the ground. Through the Fall, the very earth from which humans came, and to which humans would return, was affected.

God had given humans dominion over the earth, and they were to live off the bountiful supply of God's creation. Now, because of sin, they would have to gain the dominion through great effort and would have to live off the earth through exhausting physical labor.

2. *The entire human family fell.* Adam not only stood as the representative of the human race, he was the human race, for all coming generations were in him. When Adam fell, every man and woman who was to be born, with the one exception of Jesus Christ, fell with him.

3. *Woman was to experience sorrow and suffering in childbirth.* This was the judgment God gave to

woman. Her husband would be her leader, and she would bear children with suffering and sorrow (Genesis 3:16). Eve transgressed first and was deceived in the transgression (I Timothy 2:13-15). Adam's responsibility was greater, for he sinned deliberately and was not deceived.

D. APPLICATION OF TRUTH

Since the husband is the head, and the wife is to follow his leadership, the responsibility of the man is greater. Not only is he the breadwinner and must provide for his home and family by the sweat of his brow, but he also must take the lead in spiritual matters. He should lead in family devotions, church attendance, and teaching his family the Word of God.

Another application of this lesson is that everyone is born a sinner and needs a savior. Although he will be able to eat and gain dominion over the earth through his own efforts, he cannot possibly save himself through his own efforts.

VI. HUMANS NEED A SAVIOR

A. STATEMENT OF SCRIPTURE

1. "Behold I was shapen in iniquity; and in sin did my mother conceive me" (Psalm 51:5).

2. "And you hath he quickened, who were dead in trespasses and sins" (Ephesians 2:1).

3. "There is none righteous, no, not one" (Romans 3:10).

B. STATEMENT OF TRUTH

Since humans are dead spiritually, they cannot save themselves. They need a savior who can make them righteous, impart spiritual life to them, and restore their fellowship with God.

C. EXPOSITION OF TRUTH

Humans cannot save themselves and therefore need a savior for the following reasons:

1. *Humans are spiritually dead.* Humans are sinners, and their sin has to be atoned for. Since the result of sin is always death, the only way sin can possibly be atoned for is through death. But how can a dead person atone for sin through death, when in God's sight he is already dead? This is impossible, and another has to die for him. Since he is dead, he has to be brought to life. This again he cannot do himself; another has to do it for him.

2. *Humans have inherited a sinful nature.* Their heart is desperately wicked (Jeremiah 17:9). Their understanding is darkened (Ephesians 4:18); they are filled with all unrighteousness (Romans 1:29); and they are corrupt from head to foot (Isaiah 1:6). As such, they are sinners and they can never make themselves anything else. They cannot change themselves anymore than an Ethiopian can change his skin or a leopard his spots (Jeremiah 13:23). They might as well try to lift themselves with their own bootstraps.

3. *Human sin is rebellion against God:* Since sin is rebellion against God and a challenge to the sovereignty of God, only God Himself can forgive human sin. The sinner can never forgive or justify himself. Only the one who is sinned against can forgive and justify. In this case, it is God.

D. APPLICATION OF TRUTH

The human condition, outside of Jesus Christ, is hopeless. The unregenerate person is helpless, hopeless, and eternally lost. If he is to be saved at all, he must be saved by a source outside himself. Good works can never save a person, for these can never make him a new creation. Jesus Christ is humanity's one and only hope of salvation.

QUESTIONS

1. State at least two reasons why we know the theory of evolution is false.
2. What are four ways in which humans were created in the image of God?
3. Explain the only way in which the physical appearance of humans could be in the image of God.
4. How do we know that Adam was created innocent?
5. What were the steps that preceded the fall of humanity?
6. What is always the result of sin?
7. Explain the difference between physical death and spiritual death.
8. Explain how the entire human family fell with Adam.
9. Can humans ever save themselves? Give an explanation for your answer.
10. What is the human condition outside of Christ?

PROJECTS

1. Write a paper of at least five hundred words on the subject of sin.
2. Write a complete comparison of the temptation of our first parents with that of Christ in the wilderness.

NOTES

Chapter 3

Christ Provides Salvation

I. ONLY THE BLOOD OF A SINLESS SACRIFICE COULD ATONE FOR SIN

A. STATEMENT OF SCRIPTURE

1. "Without shedding of blood is no remission" (Hebrews 9:22).

2. "For it is the blood that maketh an atonement for the soul" (Leviticus 17:11).

3. "When I see the blood, I will pass over you" (Exodus 12:13).

B. STATEMENT OF TRUTH

The only way that sin can be atoned for is by the shedding of the blood of a perfect sacrifice. Humans could not save themselves. Therefore God had to provide the atoning sacrifice for humanity.

C. EXPOSITION OF TRUTH

The shedding of blood, of course, speaks of death. Life is in the blood (Leviticus 17:14). Therefore, when blood is spilled, life is given. For this reason, the shedding of blood makes atonement for sin.

Sin does violence to the constitution under which God and humans live. Sin is rebellion against God and is an attack against God's honor and holiness. Sin is a challenge to the sovereignty of God, for in sinning, humans choose to be a law to themselves and to deify themselves. But more than one God is an impossibility. If God could tolerate or condone sin in any measure, He no longer would be sovereign Deity. The attack against His honor and the challenge to His sovereignty demand the destruction of the sinner. Therefore, the wages of sin is always death, and the soul that sins shall die. As a result, the only way in which the honor of God can be satisfied and sin can be atoned for is through death, which is represented in the shedding of blood.

The necessity of the Atonement is based upon God's holiness and human sinfulness. God is absolutely pure and holy; He cannot tolerate or have fellowship with sin. Sin separates humans from their Creator and breaks the fellowship that God longs for. The reaction of a holy God to the awfulness of sin is described as God's wrath. This wrath can only be appeased by the destruction of both sin and the fallen nature that sins. There can be no compromise with sin. Calvary revealed the awfulness of sin and declared that God never has been, nor ever can be, indifferent to human sin.

In providing a sacrifice for the salvation of sinful humanity, God had to provide a sinless sacrifice. There had to be One offered up who had no sin, who did not deserve death for His own sins, for only such a sinless One could be a perfect atoning sacrifice for others. This God succeeded in doing by providing the Lamb of God on Calvary's cross. He was sinless and did not need to die for His own sins; therefore His blood could atone for the sins of others.

In providing salvation for sinful humanity there were a number of things God had to accomplish, including the following: (a) to handle the sin question in a way that would be consistent with His justice and that would appease His wrath; (b) to make humans holy without taking away their free moral agency; and (c) to bridge the breach between God and humans and restore the lost fellowship. All this God succeeded in doing at Calvary.

D. APPLICATION OF TRUTH

Humans can never justify themselves through good works or by being religious. In order to be saved they must accept, believe, and obey the gospel, which permits them to receive the atonement of the shed blood of the Christ of Calvary.

E. DEFINITION OF TERM

Atonement: The word "atonement" in the Hebrew literally means "covering." Atonement includes the covering of both the sins and the sinner. To atone for sin is to cover sin from God's sight so that it loses its power to provoke His wrath.

II. THE ATONEMENT WAS PROMISED FROM THE BEGINNING

A. STATEMENT OF SCRIPTURE

1. "It shall bruise thy head, and thou shalt bruise his heel" (Genesis 3:15).

2. "Unto Adam also and to his wife did the LORD God make coats of skins, and clothed them" (Genesis 3:21).

3. "The . . . blood of Christ . . . foreordained before the foundation of the world . . ." (I Peter 1:19-20).

4. "The Lamb slain from the foundation of the world . . ." (Revelation 13:8).

B. STATEMENT OF TRUTH

Calvary was from the very beginning in the plan and mind of God. As soon as our first parents fell, God promised salvation at Calvary.

C. EXPOSITION OF TRUTH

We shall study this truth under three headings that

bring out three distinct steps in God's promise of salvation:

1. *Foreknowledge of God.* God foreknew that humans would sin and in His mind and plan made provision for their salvation. In this sense God foreknew the need and made provision for it. Because of this, Jesus Christ was the Lamb slain from the foundation of the world. Actually the birth and death of Christ took place at definite dates in time, but in eternity, God saw them from the beginning.

2. *Promise of a savior.* In passing judgment upon the serpent, God declared that there would be enmity between the serpent and the woman, between its seed and her seed, that the serpent would bruise His heel and He would bruise the serpent's head (Genesis 3:15). Here the Lord God gave the first promise of Calvary. The "seed of the woman" speaks of Christ's being born of a virgin. Only by a virgin conceiving by the Holy Ghost, and the child being God manifested in the flesh, could a sinless sacrifice be provided. The seed of humanity would always be sinful and fallen and would need a savior.

The bruising of Christ's heel refers to Calvary, and the bruising of the serpent's head foretells the ultimate and final victory over Satan.

3. *A type of the Atonement was provided in the clothing of Adam and Eve.* Several points are evident in the Lord's provision of clothing for our first parents. Certainly it teaches the shame of nakedness and that humans should be clothed. However, the most important truth here is that death and the shedding of blood were necessary to clothe them. Thus God Himself began the crimson line of blood that runs consistently through the Scriptures.

D. APPLICATION OF TRUTH

God will do for humans what they cannot do for themselves. We shall see in a later study that God will not do what He expects humans to do for themselves, and He holds humans responsible for obedience to the gospel. However, when humanity was helpless in providing an atonement for sin, God provided the remedy. In the same manner He will not only save us but will answer our prayers today. He never changes!

E. DEFINITION OF TERMS

1. *Foreknowledge:* This term helps us to understand that God knows the future from the beginning. Actually God, who dwells in eternity, has an ever-present knowledge. He ever sees both the past and future as one eternal present.

2. *Seed of the woman*: The humanity of Jesus Christ; the flesh that was born of Mary to be offered on Calvary as the Lamb of God.

III. THE ATONEMENT WAS BROUGHT ABOUT BY LOVE

A. STATEMENT OF SCRIPTURE

1. "For God so loved the world, that he gave his only begotten Son, that whosoever believeth in him should not perish, but have everlasting life" (John 3:16).

2. "But God commendeth his love toward us, in that, while we were yet sinners, Christ died for us" (Romans 5:8).

3. "Hereby perceive we the love of God, because he laid down his life for us" (I John 3:16).

B. STATEMENT OF TRUTH

The reason that God provided salvation for humanity through the death of Christ on Calvary was that He loved humanity. There may have been secondary reasons that influenced the decision of the Lord in planning the remedy for sin, but the greatest and chief thing that caused

Him to provide salvation was that God loved humanity with an infinite and inexhaustible love.

C. EXPOSITION OF TRUTH

The whole of Scripture proves that love, simply and solely, motivated God to provide the sacrificial Lamb of God on Calvary's cross to save sinful humanity.

Not only does God love humanity, but God is love (I John 4:16). Love is the very essence of His nature. In spite of human wickedness and rebellion, God still loves the sinner and endeavors to save him from his wickedness. He has the best interest of humans at heart. He longs to make them His children through the new birth and restore them to full fellowship with Himself. This was possible only through the Atonement. Christ's sufferings and death on the cross of Calvary are the highest expression of God's love for humanity.

Calvary proves that God loves the entire world, the whole human race, all individuals of all nationalities.

D. APPLICATION OF TRUTH

Such wonderful love of God, which spared not His highest and best, should win our love to the degree that we are more than willing to dedicate to Him our best, our all, our life.

Moreover, since God loves all people everywhere, and the love of God is shed abroad in our hearts (Romans 5:5), then we should love our fellow humans everywhere.

IV. THE SUBSTITUTIONARY DEATH OF CHRIST DID EVERYTHING THAT NEEDED TO BE DONE

A. STATEMENT OF SCRIPTURE

1. "For he hath made him to be sin for us, who knew no sin" (II Corinthians 5:21).

2. "Who his own self bare our sins in his own body on the tree" (I Peter 2:24).

3. "Ye were not redeemed with corruptible things . . . but with the precious blood of Christ, as of a lamb without blemish and without spot" (I Peter 1:18-19).

4. "God was in Christ, reconciling the world unto himself" (II Corinthians 5:19).

B. STATEMENT OF TRUTH

Whatever was necessary to deal with the sin question and to reconcile humans to God was accomplished at Calvary. The death of Christ on the cross is the propitiation for sin. It redeems sinful humans from the bondage of sin and reconciles them to a holy God.

C. EXPOSITION OF TRUTH

The Atonement is a large subject about which volumes could be written. We shall content ourselves with a brief summary under four headings, which should help us to understand the magnitude and scope of the accomplishments of Calvary.

1. *Substitution.* The death of Jesus Christ was vicarious; He died in our stead. Just as the ram caught in the thicket was a substitute for Isaac on Mount Moriah, even so was Christ a substitute for each of us. Just as Barabbas was set free by the death of Christ, even so each of us may be set free. We must recognize that Christ died in the place of each individual, not only for the world collectively. (See Isaiah 53:4-8.)

2. *Propitiation.* The righteous wrath of a holy God was appeased by the offering of an atoning sacrifice on Calvary's cross. For God to be God He must judge sin, and we know definitely that He will judge all sin. Calvary provides a place of judgment where the penalty for our sins is meted out. Through faith in and obedience to the gospel, our sins are judged here and we may go free.

3. *Redemption.* Sinful humans are in bondage to sin and death. To free them from the bondage of sin they had to be redeemed by payment of the proper price. Jesus Christ is our Redeemer, and His atoning work is our redemption. In the Old Testament, when someone wanted to redeem a person from bondage, the redeemer had to have certain qualifications: (a) he had be kin to the person who needed to be redeemed; (b) he had to be willing to redeem by paying the price; and (c) he had to have the price.

Jesus Christ measured up to all three of these qualifications. We are redeemed with the price that was paid—the precious blood of Christ.

4. *Reconciliation.* Fellowship between God and humanity was broken by human disobedience. God is not reconciled to humanity, but rather God did something to reconcile humans to Himself. God bridged the breach so that humans now have the privilege of crossing over to full fellowship. This act of reconciliation is a finished work. Christ's death has made the reconciliation of all humanity possible; each individual must make it actual in his own life.

D. APPLICATION OF TRUTH

There is nothing that humans can add to make their redemption more complete. The price has been paid; the work has been accomplished. This proves conclusively that humans are saved by grace and grace alone. In other words, humans only need to accept the provision of salvation, believe it, obey the conditions of the gospel, and enter into eternal life.

E. DEFINITION OF TERMS

1. *Vicarious*: Performing or suffering in the place of another.

2. *Propitiation*: This word is believed to come from

the Latin word *prope*, meaning "near." Propitiation means a sacrifice of atonement, appeasement of wrath, satisfaction of justice. The sacrifice of Calvary brings humans near to God by appeasing His righteous wrath and satisfying His justice.

3. *Redeem*: To buy back by paying a price; to loose from bondage by paying a price; to buy in a market.

V. THE BLOOD OF CHRIST IS FULLY EFFICACIOUS BUT IS ONLY EFFECTIVE WHERE IT IS APPLIED

A. STATEMENT OF SCRIPTURE

1. "How much more shall the blood of Christ, who through the eternal Spirit offered himself without spot to God, purge your conscience from dead works to serve the living God?" (Hebrews 9:14).

2. "The blood of Jesus Christ his Son cleanseth us from all sin" (I John 1:7).

3. "And they shall take of the blood, and strike it on the two side posts and on the upper door posts of the houses. . . . When I see the blood, I will pass over you" (Exodus 12:7, 13).

B. STATEMENT OF TRUTH

There is power in the shed blood of Christ to cleanse the vilest sinner, and there is no lack in the efficacy of the Atonement. However, the blood has no effect where it is not applied; only through faith in and obedience to the gospel can the sinner receive the effects of the saving virtue of the blood of Christ.

C. EXPOSITION OF TRUTH

On the evening of the Passover the Israelites killed a lamb as God commanded, but it would have done them no good if they had not been in the house with the blood applied to the lintel and door post. It was the application of the blood that saved them when the death angel passed over. Even so, it is the application of the blood that saves today. God has provided a sure remedy for sin, but for it to be effective in our lives we must apply it personally.

Medical science may discover a drug that will cure a certain disease, but it is absolutely no use if it is not given to the suffering one. The same principle is true in regard to salvation from sin.

The Atonement is the theme of the Bible. It is the scarlet cord running through every page of God's Word. One out of every forty-four verses in the New Testament speaks of the Atonement. It was the subject of the conversation of Moses and Elijah on the Mount of Transfiguration (Luke 9:30-31); it is the theme of the song in heaven (Revelation 5:8-12). However, all of this means nothing if the blood is not applied; it cannot meet the need of the sinner who does not meet the conditions of the gospel.

D. APPLICATION OF TRUTH

Some people say we are to do nothing to be saved. This is a false presentation of the gospel. If we do nothing, we shall end up lost in eternity. While we cannot contribute to our salvation, we can and must meet the conditions of the offer of salvation. A surgeon may perform a life-saving operation, but the patient must first present himself for the operation. A pilot may fly a passenger to his destination, but the passenger must first board the airplane. Likewise, there is something for the sinner to do before he can be saved. He must meet the conditions of the gospel before the blood of Christ can become efficacious to him.

God has provided a remedy for sin. It took the death, burial, and resurrection of our Lord to provide this remedy. For this remedy to be effective in our lives, we must identify personally with Him in death, burial, and resurrection.

E. DEFINITION OF TERM

Efficacious: Producing or sure to produce a desired result.

VI. THE ATONING DEATH OF CHRIST WAS VALIDATED BY HIS RESURRECTION

A. STATEMENT OF SCRIPTURE

1. "Who was delivered for our offences, and was raised again for our justification" (Romans 4:25).

2. "And if Christ be not risen, then is our preaching vain, and your faith is also vain" (I Corinthians 15:14).

3. "And declared to be the Son of God with power, according to the spirit of holiness, by the resurrection from the dead" (Romans 1:4).

B. STATEMENT OF TRUTH

The resurrection of Jesus Christ gives value to His atoning work. It shows that God accepts the atoning blood of Christ, and it is therefore efficacious to wash away sin. It proves the deity of Jesus, who is living and ever present. Because He arose, the penitent sinner, through the new birth, may also rise to walk in newness of life. The resurrection of Christ makes eternal life certain and gives the child of God the hope of his own resurrection.

C. EXPOSITION OF TRUTH

In the Old Testament the people waited outside the Temple for the high priest to come out of the Holy Place, for they knew then that all their sins were borne away. Our high priest came out of the grave, and by this we know that His blood was accepted and that our sins were atoned for. We now know that the sin question is settled, and through obedience to the gospel we shall be justified. Because of this, the resurrection of Jesus Christ gives value to His atoning sacrifice.

In order for salvation to be a reality in the life of a believer it is necessary that there be a living Savior. A dead Savior could do nothing to help the dead. It takes a living Savior to forgive, to lift, to heal, to regenerate, to give power to overcome Satan. There certainly would be no power to save in His Word or His name if He were dead. It took His resurrection to give power to the gospel message and permit salvation to become a reality in the life of an individual.

The resurrection of Jesus Christ proves the reality of the new birth. Even as Christ rose from the dead, so those who are dead in sin can rise to walk in newness of life.

Finally, the hope of salvation is eternal life and spending eternity in heaven. If Jesus Christ had not risen, there could be no possibility of a resurrection to eternal life. Our hope of the resurrection is based squarely upon the fact of His resurrection, as the apostle Paul made plain (I Corinthians 15).

D. APPLICATION OF TRUTH

In order to experience salvation we must experience the power of the resurrection in our lives. The resurrection proves the essentiality of the new birth.

The death, burial, and resurrection of Christ were all essential in His work of providing salvation. A child of God must identify with Christ and be in Christ (I Corinthians 15:22). The whole human race fell when Adam fell, for they were all in Adam. Likewise those who are made alive must be in Christ. As it took death, burial, and resurrection to bring salvation, so it will take death, burial, and resurrection to enter into salvation. As Adam fell through unbelief and disobedience, the child of God will be saved through faith and obedience. It is through faith in and obedience to the gospel that a person can experience death, burial, and resurrection and be saved.

QUESTIONS

1. What is the meaning of the word "atonement" ?
2. Why was the Atonement necessary?
3. Explain how Jesus Christ was "the Lamb slain from the foundation of the world."
4. What motivated God in providing the Atonement?
5. How did Jesus meet the qualifications of a redeemer?
6. To what extent is the blood of Christ efficacious?
7. What is the meaning of the term "propitiation"?
8. Where may our sins be judged?
9. Why is the resurrection of Jesus Christ important to the Atonement?
10. Give an Old Testament type of the substitutionary death of Christ.

PROJECTS

1. Using a concordance, trace the crimson line of blood that runs through the Scriptures.
2. Write an explanation (at least three hundred words in length) of Genesis 3:15.

NOTES

Chapter 4
Repentance (Death)

I. FAITH IS ESSENTIAL TO SALVATION

A. STATEMENT OF SCRIPTURE

1. "He that believeth and is baptized shall be saved" (Mark 16:16).

2. "And they said, Believe on the Lord Jesus Christ, and thou shalt be saved, and thy house" (Acts 16:31).

3. "For with the heart man believeth unto righteousness" (Romans 10:10).

4. "For by grace are ye saved through faith" (Ephesians 2:8).

B. STATEMENT OF TRUTH

Faith is absolutely essential to salvation. Unless a person believes on the Lord Jesus Christ he cannot be saved.

C. EXPOSITION OF TRUTH

The Bible makes it very clear that the penitent sinner must believe in his heart before he can be saved. Saving faith is the open door through which God extends grace to a sinner; the hand that reaches out to receive and appropriate the mercy of God is saving faith.

1. *Why is faith essential*? Our first parents fell in the Garden through unbelief and disobedience. Even so, we must be saved through faith and obedience. The sacrificial

atonement of Calvary provides salvation for a sinner. However, before it can become efficacious in the life of an individual he must recognize, accept, and receive it with a saving faith. Each person is still a free moral agent. He must accept and receive Jesus Christ into his heart through his own personal decision and acceptance. He hears the gospel, which is the message of the death, burial, and resurrection of Jesus Christ. He accepts and believes the gospel in his heart. Thus he receives God's grace and mercy; there is no other way. (See John 1:12; Romans 10:9; Hebrews 11:6.)

2. *What is saving faith*? The faith that saves is a living faith that works. It is not just mental assent. A person may give intellectual assent to the gospel without committing his life to it. Saving faith is the commitment of the entire personality, involving intellect, emotion, and will. Saving faith is a faith unto obedience. If one believes to the saving of his soul, he repents and obeys the gospel. Without repentance and obedience, it is impossible for one to believe with a saving faith. Faith, repentance, and obedience are all necessary and essential to salvation. We cannot have two of these without having the third. Therefore, saving faith is a faith unto obedience.

3. *What is the source of faith*? Faith is a gift of God's grace. God desires to impart faith in the heart of all, and He will do so if they do not resist Him. We are not so much responsible for lacking faith as we are for resisting and rejecting Jesus Christ and failing to place our faith in Him. As we receive Him, faith springs up in our hearts (John 1:12; Hebrews 12:2).

Faith is based upon the Word of God. Hearing the gospel and permitting the Word to lodge in our hearts is the greatest source of faith. Saving faith is the direct result of receiving the Word of God into the heart (Romans 10:17).

In receiving salvation the order is (a) fact, (b) faith, (c) feeling. We may state the steps in receiving salvation as follows: (a) hearing the gospel, (b) conviction of sin, (c) faith, (d) repentance, (e) obedience, (f) blessing.

D. APPLICATION OF TRUTH

Since saving faith is always accompanied by repentance and obedience, the person who accepts salvation and believes to the saving of his soul will repent and be baptized in the name of Jesus. We have the right to question an individual as to whether or not he truly believes if he refuses to be baptized in Jesus' name.

II. OBEDIENCE IS ESSENTIAL TO SALVATION

A. STATEMENT OF SCRIPTURE

1. "And so is also the Holy Ghost, whom God hath given to them that obey Him" (Acts 5:32).
2. "Whether of sin unto death, or of obedience unto righteousness" (Romans 6:16).
3. "In flaming fire taking vengeance on them that know not God, and that obey not the gospel of our Lord Jesus Christ" (II Thessalonians 1:8).

B. STATEMENT OF TRUTH

Obedience to the gospel is absolutely essential to salvation. It is impossible for someone to be saved unless he obeys the truth.

C. EXPOSITION OF TRUTH

Disobedience brought about the fall of humanity. Disobedience is a direct challenge to the sovereignty of God, a deliberate rebellion to the revealed will of God, and a deification of humanity. At the root of all sin is the spirit of self-will and disobedience. Because of this, God will judge all disobedience (Romans 5:18-19; Hebrews 2:2; I Timothy 1:9).

Just as disobedience ends with judgment and death, so obedience to the gospel results in eternal life. Adam was disobedient, and in him we all fell; Jesus Christ was obedient (Philippians 2:8), and if we are in Him, we shall also be obedient and live. It is impossible to be in Christ unless we are willing to be obedient to the gospel.

There is only one gospel that will save a soul. There is only one way, which was provided at Calvary. There is the clear choice of either accepting and obeying this one message of truth or continuing down the broad road to a lost eternity. There is no neutral ground. There is no way to have peace with God except by surrendering, submitting our wills to His, and obeying.

D. APPLICATION OF TRUTH

The main application of this truth is that a sinner who believes and obeys the gospel will repent and be baptized in the name of Jesus Christ. There will be many places where obedience is called for. Holiness will follow conversion, and it involves a life of obedience. However, so far as the act of a sinner accepting salvation is concerned, obedience demands repentance and baptism by immersion in the name of Jesus.

III. REPENTANCE IS ESSENTIAL TO SALVATION

A. STATEMENT OF SCRIPTURE

1. "I tell you, Nay: but, except ye repent, ye shall all likewise perish" (Luke 13:3).

2. "And the times of this ignorance God winked at; but now commandeth all men every where to repent" (Acts 17:30).

3. "But is longsuffering to us-ward, not willing that any should perish, but that all should come to repentance" (II Peter 3:9).

B. STATEMENT OF TRUTH

Without repentance it is absolutely impossible for a

sinner to receive forgiveness of sins.

C. EXPOSITION OF TRUTH

The importance of repentance to salvation may be seen by the following facts:

1. John the Baptist preached repentance (Matthew 3:1-2).
2. Jesus preached repentance (Matthew 4:17).
3. Jesus commanded the twelve apostles to preach it (Luke 24:47).
4. Jesus commanded the seventy disciples to preach it (Luke 10:9).
5. Peter preached repentance (Acts 2:38).
6. Paul preached repentance (Acts 20:21).

Our Lord gave the apostle Peter the keys to the kingdom (Matthew 16:19). On the Day of Pentecost, when Peter told the people how to be saved, the first thing he instructed them to do was to repent (Acts 2:38).

We can clearly understand the place of repentance in the plan of salvation if we recognize that repentance identifies the individual with Christ in death. There can be no burial and resurrection until there is first a death. Therefore, repentance is the true basis for the birth of water and Spirit. Water baptism is meaningless if it is not first preceded by genuine repentance.

Faith and repentance are both essential to salvation, and it is impossible to have saving faith without repentance. Faith and repentance will be accompanied by obedience to the gospel, which will cause the penitent to desire to be baptized.

D. APPLICATION OF TRUTH

As soon as a person repents he is ready for water baptism. There should be no unnecessary delay, although he should never be baptized until he has fully repented (Acts 8:36-38).

IV. REPENTANCE AFFECTS A PERSON'S ENTIRE BEING

A. STATEMENT OF SCRIPTURE

1. "How shall we, that are dead to sin, live any longer therein?" (Romans 6:2).

2. "Thou fool, that which thou sowest is not quickened, except it die" (I Corinthians 15:36).

3. "Ye sorrowed to repentance; for ye were made sorry after a godly manner" (II Corinthians 7:9).

4. "Let the wicked forsake his way, and the unrighteous man his thoughts; and let him return unto the LORD, and he will have mercy upon him" (Isaiah 55:7).

B. STATEMENT OF TRUTH

A person's entire nature is affected by repentance; his intellect, his emotions, his will, and his very being are influenced by the act of repentance. His life is completely changed when he fully repents.

C. EXPOSITION OF TRUTH

Just as salvation saves the entire person, so repentance changes a person's entire being and nature. It turns him about-face and inside out, completely revolutionizing his life, and it qualifies him for regeneration.

1. *Repentance is a death to sin, self, and the world.* It was necessary for Jesus Christ to die, be buried, and rise again in order to provide salvation. It is necessary for the sinner to experience death, burial, and resurrection in order to receive salvation. Repentance is death to sin and the world (Romans 6:2-4). If we are to be "in Christ" we must experience both death and resurrection in Christ. Even as Christ's body was crucified, so the church is a crucified body and can never experience the power of His resurrection until it experiences death through repentance.

Much of the struggling that we sometimes see in people

who seek for the Holy Ghost is due to the process of dying. When a person has fully repented, the power of sin is broken, there is a full surrender to the will of God, and the way is clear for the seeker to be filled with the Holy Ghost.

2. *Repentance affects the intellect.* The act of repentance brings about a change of mind (Matthew 21:29). In fact, this change of mind is a complete renewal (Romans 12:2).

3. *Repentance affects the emotions.* Repentance is a godly sorrow (II Corinthians 7:7-11). There must be a certain amount of heart sorrow, even if there is little evidence of it outwardly. The tax collector beat upon his breast, indicating sorrow (Luke 18:13). However, the heart must not only be broken because of sin but the heart must be broken from sin.

4. *Repentance affects the human will.* Being sorry is not sufficient, for the sinner must forsake what he wishes God to remit. He makes a decision and turns from sin. Not only does he turn from sin but he turns to Jesus. The prodigal not only was sorry but he arose and turned his footsteps homeward. Like the prodigal, the penitent sinner will confess his sin, forsake sin, and turn to Jesus Christ (Luke 18:13; Proverbs 28:13; Acts 26:18).

D. APPLICATION OF TRUTH

When a person is still a servant of sin he has not repented of that sin. For example, if he still smokes he has not repented of smoking. When he repents he will see smoking as sinful, he will have a sorrow because of it, and will die to it. It may be a struggle, but when repentance is complete he will be dead to the habit of smoking.

V. REPENTANCE COMES BY VARIOUS MEANS

A. STATEMENT OF SCRIPTURE

1. "The goodness of God leadeth thee to repentance" (Romans 2:4).

2. "In meekness instructing those that oppose themselves; if God peradventure will give them repentance" (II Timothy 2:25).

B. STATEMENT OF TRUTH

God uses many means in dealing with sinners to bring them to repentance. Repentance originates with God, but a person is responsible to yield to the dealings of God and repent.

C. EXPOSITION OF TRUTH

One of the greatest forces that God uses to melt the hard heart of sinners is His own love and goodness (Romans 2:4; II Peter 3:9). With others He has to use chastisement and reproof (Revelation 3:19; II Timothy 2:24-25). Possibly the greatest means He uses is the preaching of the gospel in the power of the Holy Ghost (Jonah 3:5-10; I Thessalonians 1:5-10).

Just as fire hardens clay and melts wax, so God's dealings with humans have different results. It is God's will that everyone repent, and He uses many means to bring it about. Humans are responsible for their own response to the Word of God and God's dealings with them. They can harden their hearts and be lost, or they can humble themselves, repent, and be saved.

Some people surrender to the gospel almost immediately and repent within a few minutes. Others have to be dealt with over a long period of time; for them repentance is a long, slow process, taking many days to complete.

D. APPLICATION OF TRUTH

The important thing is not the length of time it takes to repent but that repentance is deep and genuine.

Since everyone of us is different, none can measure his own experience with that of another. One may repent, be immersed in water in Jesus' name, and receive the

Holy Ghost all in one evening. Another may take many days before the work is complete. The important and essential thing is that a person yield fully to the dealings of God and make certain that the work of repentance is complete in his life.

VI. THE RESULTS OF REPENTANCE ARE MANY

A. STATEMENT OF SCRIPTURE

1. "Likewise I say unto you, there is joy in the presence of the angels of God over one sinner that repenteth" (Luke 15:1).

2. "Let the wicked forsake his way, and the unrighteous man his thoughts; and let him return unto the LORD, and he will have mercy upon him; and to our God, for he will abundantly pardon" (Isaiah 55:7).

3. "Repent ye therefore, and be converted, that your sins may be blotted out, when the times of refreshing shall come from the presence of the Lord" (Acts 3:1).

B. STATEMENT OF TRUTH

A genuine work of repentance in the heart of a penitent sinner brings many results. These are the fruits worthy of repentance (Matthew 3:8), which are the evidences of repentance itself. True repentance, which produces such fruit, qualifies an individual for full New Testament salvation.

C. EXPOSITION OF TRUTH

When John the Baptist saw the Pharisees come to the Jordan River, he exhorted them to bring forth fruits worthy of repentance. His admonition shows that repentance is to be accompanied by definite results that will be evidence of repentance. A mere religious profession is not sufficient. There must be certain works and results that will prove that repentance has taken place. The work of true repentance is far-reaching and brings about many results, among which will be the desire to be baptized in the name of Jesus and receive the gift of the Holy Ghost (Acts 2:38). We shall mention a few of the effects of genuine, heartfelt repentance.

1. *Repentance brings obedience to the gospel.* A sinner has a heart of disobedience. He rebels at the will of God in His life and refuses to obey the gospel. When he repents he desires the will of God and immediately seeks to obey the gospel. This change of heart causes him to desire to be baptized in the name of Jesus Christ, to receive the Holy Ghost, and to live a holy life. Repentance will result in a life of obedience, of observing all that Christ has commanded us (Matthew 28:20).

2. *Repentance brings restitution.* The penitent sinner can do very little about the great majority of his past sins except to bring them to Jesus Christ and to behold the Lamb of God who takes away the sins of the world. However, in everyone's life there are generally a few mistakes that he can correct. Honor and moral principles call for restitution insofar as it is possible. We should not expect the Lord to forgive a sin that we can correct if we refuse to do so. For example, if a person has stolen money, he should repay it. If he has lied about someone's character, he should endeavor to right the wrong done. We see this principle in the experience of Zacchaeus. His repentance included restitution (Luke 19:1-10).

Before leaving this subject, let us give a word of caution. A sinner's life is generally so entangled that only God can untangle most of the knots. Usually, the Lord will bring to the penitent's mind a few small things that he can make straight. These may simply be tests of his change of heart and his sincerity. He should recognize that there are many things he can never correct, and if he were to try he would only make them worse. Marital and moral problems generally fall in this category. In these matters the only thing for the penitent to do is to look to the Lord to remit the past and then leave it under the blood.

3. *Repentance brings confession of sin.* Confession of sin goes hand in hand with repentance. David confessed his sin before he could find pardon (II Samuel 12:13; Psalm 51). The prodigal returned home, confessing his sin (Luke 15:21). There is a definite promise of forgiveness to the one who confesses (Proverbs 28:13; I John 1:9). However, we must remember that this confession is to Jesus Christ, our high priest. There may be times when repentance will demand that confession be made to an individual who has been wronged. As in the case of restitution, there is very little that a person can do about most of his past, except to confess it to Jesus Christ and then leave it under the blood.

4. *Repentance brings a birth of the Word.* Jesus compared regeneration to the natural birth when He told Nicodemus that he must be born again. Jesus used the expression "born of water and of the Spirit" (John 3:5). In the Epistles we find passages that speak of being born of the Word (James 1:18; I Peter 1:23; I Corinthians 4:15).

The best way to have a clear understanding of the new birth is to compare it with the natural birth, even as Jesus did. In both there are three distinct phases:

Natural birth: (a) conception—planting the seed; (b) physical birth—birth of water; (c) breath enters the newborn babe.

Spiritual birth: (a) hearing and believing the gospel, with repentance; (b) water baptism in the name of Jesus; (c) baptism of the Holy Ghost.

Undoubtedly, the Word of God being planted in the heart of the hearer is one of the divine agencies that brings about repentance. Yet it is also true that repentance permits the gospel seed to germinate and spring up to life eternal.

5. *Repentance will qualify a person for pardon and regeneration.* A person does not earn forgiveness by repenting, but repentance is a condition for receiving forgiveness. Repentance qualifies a person for pardon, but it does not entitle him to it (apart from the grace of God). (See Acts 3:19; Isaiah 55:7.) Repentance also qualifies a person for regeneration—for water baptism and the gift of the Holy Ghost (Acts 2:38).

D. APPLICATION OF TRUTH

We have every right to expect the foregoing results to follow true repentance. If there are no fruits of repentance, we may seriously question whether or not one has fully repented. If a person refuses to walk in light and to obey revealed truth, it is quite evident that he has not fully repented.

QUESTIONS

1. Why is faith essential to salvation?
2. Why is obedience essential to salvation?
3. Why is repentance essential to salvation?
4. Explain what is meant by "saving faith."
5. What is the source of faith?
6. Explain fully the meaning of repentance.
7. What are the effects of true repentance?
8. How is repentance produced?
9. How may we know when one has repented?
10. What connection does restitution have with repentance?

PROJECTS

1. List all the examples of repentance that you can find (a) in the Old Testament; (b) in the four Gospels; (c) in the Book of Acts

2. Write an explanation (at least three hundred words)

of how faith, obedience, and repentance work together to bring salvation to a person's life.

NOTES

Chapter 5

Christian Baptism in Jesus' Name (Burial)

I. WATER BAPTISM IS ESSENTIAL TO NEW TESTAMENT SALVATION

A. STATEMENT OF SCRIPTURE

1. "He that believeth and is baptized shall be saved" (Mark 16:16).

2. "The like figure whereunto even baptism doth also now save us" (I Peter 3:21).

B. STATEMENT OF TRUTH

The ordinance of water baptism in the name of Jesus has an essential place in full salvation. In order to be ready for the return of our Lord, it is necessary to be baptized.

C. EXPOSITION OF TRUTH

We may see the importance of water baptism in the plan of salvation when we study the significance of both the mode and the formula of baptism.

1. *Mode.* The Greek verb *baptizo,* from which we get the English word *baptize,* means fundamentally to "dip, plunge, immerse." The word *baptism* properly and literally means "immersion." The Bible makes very clear that the proper mode of baptism is by immersion in water. (See Acts 8:38.) This biblical mode of baptism has great

significance. By immersion one is identified with Christ in burial (Romans 6:4). Only by being immersed in water can the meaning of a burial be experienced. Thus the mode of baptism reveals the importance of baptism in the plan of salvation.

2. *Formula.* Without exception, the early church always administered baptism in the name of Jesus. At baptism one is baptized "into" the name of Jesus, which is the saving name of our God. There is salvation in no other name. Acts 4:12 plainly and emphatically states this truth: "Neither is there salvation in any other: for there is none other name under heaven given among men, whereby we must be saved." The Bible states plainly that remission of sins is in the name of Jesus (Luke 24:47; Acts 2:38). If both salvation and remission of sins are in the name of Jesus, we can readily see how the formula reveals the importance of baptism in the plan of salvation.

Jesus stated that in order to be saved a person would have to believe and be baptized (Mark 16:16). In Paul's letter to Titus we find another statement regarding the importance of baptism in salvation: "According to his mercy he saved us, by the washing of regeneration, and renewing of the Holy Ghost" (Titus 3:5). The term "washing of regeneration" literally means "bath of regeneration," and most ancient and modern commentators have interpreted it to mean baptism.

The essential place that water baptism has in the plan of salvation can readily be proved further by many more passages of Scripture. However, these should be sufficient to satisfy every honest soul seeking for truth.

D. APPLICATION OF TRUTH

Since water baptism is essential, there is no place for argument, and the seeking soul has no choice but to obey. It is not something for him to reject or accept according to his own whim. As soon as he has fully repented he must obey the gospel by being baptized by immersion in water in the name of Jesus. If he has never been baptized according to the Bible it is necessary for him to do so. There is only one baptism. If either the mode or the formula is incorrect, he has not yet been baptized scripturally.

E. DEFINITION OF TERMS

1. *Ordinance*: A statute or decree given to the church by Jesus Christ that must be obeyed.

2. *Mode*: The manner in which baptism is to be practiced, which is by a single immersion in water.

3. *Formula*: The words spoken by the minister while baptizing a convert, which must state that the baptism is into the name of Jesus.

II. WATER BAPTISM IS AN IDENTIFICATION WITH CHRIST IN BURIAL

A. STATEMENT OF SCRIPTURE

1. "Therefore we are buried with him by baptism into death" (Romans 6:4).

2. "Buried with him in baptism" (Colossians 2:12).

B. STATEMENT OF TRUTH

Immersion in water is a burial and signifies an identification with Jesus Christ in death and burial.

C. EXPOSITION OF TRUTH

In order to atone for the sins of humanity it was necessary for Christ to suffer death, be buried, and rise again. If we are to be saved we must be "in Christ" (I Corinthians 15:22). This means that the penitent sinner must experience death, burial, and resurrection. In repentance, he experiences a death to sin and the world. Burial must follow death, for a dead man is never left unburied.

Water baptism is this burial. Even as burial follows death, so does water baptism (immersion in water) follow repentance. In the foregoing passages of Scripture the apostle Paul plainly stated that we are buried with Christ in baptism.

D. APPLICATION OF TRUTH

When we understand the true significance of water baptism, it would be foolish to substitute some other mode. Sprinkling and pouring can never mean burial, no matter what freedom one may give his imagination. Realizing this truth, a person has no choice but to be immersed in water if he desires to be baptized.

III. THE NAME OF JESUS IS ESSENTIAL TO WATER BAPTISM

A. STATEMENT OF SCRIPTURE

1. "Then Peter said unto them, Repent, and be baptized every one of you in the name of Jesus Christ for the remission of sins, and ye shall receive the gift of the Holy Ghost" (Acts 2:38).

2. "Only they were baptized in the name of the Lord Jesus" (Acts 8:16).

3. "Baptizing them in the name of the Father, and of the Son, and of the Holy Ghost" (Matthew 28:19).

B. STATEMENT OF TRUTH

Just as the biblical mode of baptism is essential, so the biblical formula of baptism is essential. Water baptism must be in (or more correctly, into) the name of Jesus. A person is not baptized scripturally who has never been baptized into the name of Jesus.

C. EXPOSITION OF TRUTH

The testimony of Scripture is so overwhelming on this

point that it almost seems a waste of time to develop an argument for this truth. However, knowing to what degree Satan hates the name of Jesus and attacks this glorious truth, it is wise to have a strong defense. For this reason we shall develop a number of reasons why water baptism is in the name of Jesus, any one of which is sufficient proof that this message is correct.

1. *"Jesus" is the name (singular) of the Father, Son, and Holy Ghost.* The terms Father, Son, and Holy Ghost are titles and certainly are not names. What is the name of the Father? Jesus! What is the name of the Son? Jesus! What is the name of the Holy Ghost? Jesus! The name is singular not plural. We are baptized into the name, not names. What is the name? There can be only one answer: Jesus!

2. *Scripture never contradicts itself.* Those who say that they would rather take the words of Jesus than the words of Peter admit that they believe in a contradiction of Scripture. However, both Matthew 28:19 and Acts 2:38 are right. They do not contradict one another. It is clear that a person has not obeyed Matthew 28:19 until he has been baptized according to Acts 2:38.

3. *The apostle Peter had just heard the words of Matthew 28:19 spoken a few days before.* He had just received the Holy Ghost, who was to guide him into all truth. He had been entrusted with the keys to the kingdom. Could it be possible that he made a mistake? No! Never!

4. *There are not two gospels.* Neither are there two ways to baptize. Those who argue that only Jews or Jewish proselytes were baptized in the name of Jesus are admitting that they believe in two gospels, one for the Jews and another for the Gentiles. This, of course, is ridiculous. There is but one gospel and one way to be baptized.

5. *If we accept the literal fulfillment of Acts 2:4 in the baptism of the Holy Ghost, it is also necessary that*

we accept the literal fulfillment of Acts 2:38.

6. *Remission of sins is in the name of Jesus* (Luke 24:47). How then could we use any other term, title, or name?

7. *Jesus is the saving name of our God.* There is no other name whereby we must be saved (Acts 4:12). How then can we avoid using the name of Jesus in water baptism?

8. *The family name is Jesus* (Ephesians 3:15). If we are His children we shall bear the family name.

9. *The bride takes her husband's name.* What is the bridegroom's name? Jesus! What name will the bride take upon her? Jesus!

10. *Whatever we do in word or deed we do in the name of Jesus* (Colossians 3:17). Water baptism is both word and deed.

11. *By water baptism we are identified with Jesus Christ in His death, burial, and resurrection.* Were the Father and the Holy Ghost crucified and buried in addition to Jesus?

D. APPLICATION OF TRUTH

The application is simple. In order to be baptized according to the Bible it is necessary to be baptized in the name of Jesus.

IV. THE APOSTLES ALWAYS BAPTIZED IN THE NAME OF JESUS

A. STATEMENT OF SCRIPTURE

1. "Only they were baptized in the name of the Lord Jesus" (Acts 8:16).

2. "And he commanded them to be baptized in the name of the Lord" (Acts 10:48). (See Acts 9:5.)

3. "When they heard this, they were baptized in the name of the Lord Jesus" (Acts 19:5).

B. STATEMENT OF TRUTH

The early church always baptized in the name of Jesus. The Bible does not record one exception.

C. EXPOSITION OF TRUTH

Both the record of the Bible and church history verify that the early church always, without exception, baptized in the name of Jesus. There is an abundance of material in various church histories and encyclopedias to prove this fact. However we shall content ourselves here with the biblical record.

1. *Jerusalem.* Peter was given a very special commission when Jesus said to him, "And I will give unto thee the keys of the kingdom of heaven" (Matthew 16:19). The apostle Peter used the keys for the first time when he preached the gospel on the Day of Pentecost and about three thousand souls entered the kingdom. The other eleven disciples (including Matthew) stood with Peter, confirming and agreeing with the message that Peter preached (Acts 2:14). When the multitude cried out to the apostles, "Men and brethren, what shall we do?" Peter answered with the authority of all heaven behind him, "Repent, and be baptized every one of you in the name of Jesus Christ for the remission of sins, and ye shall receive the gift of the Holy Ghost" (Acts 2:38).

2. *Samaria.* Philip preached Christ to Samaria, and great joy came to that city. The Samaritans believed the things concerning the kingdom of God and the name of Jesus Christ, and they were baptized in the name of the Lord Jesus (Acts 8:12, 16).

3. *Damascus.* Saul of Tarsus obeyed the message that Ananias brought to him. "And now why tarriest thou? arise and be baptized, and wash away thy sins, calling on the name of the Lord" (Acts 22:16).

4. *Caesarea.* In the home of Cornelius, the apostle Peter commanded the Gentiles to be baptized in the name

of the Lord (Acts 10:48). Most modern translations state the name of Jesus Christ here. The *New English Bible* says, "Then he ordered them to be baptized in the name of Jesus Christ."

5. *Ephesus.* The apostle Paul found disciples who had been baptized unto John's baptism. It was necessary for them to be baptized in the name of the Lord Jesus. They obeyed and received the Holy Ghost (Acts 19:1-6).

6. *Corinth.* Paul's first epistle to the Corinthians makes it very clear that they too were baptized in the name of Jesus. "Is Christ divided? was Paul crucified for you? or were ye baptized in the name of Paul?" (I Corinthians 1:13). Who was crucified for the Corinthians? Into whose name were they baptized? There can be but one answer: Jesus Christ!

Is there even one exception to this scriptural record? There is not a single exception. Nowhere is there even a hint or an inference that the early church baptized any other way.

D. APPLICATION OF TRUTH

Seldom does any truth have such a weight of scriptural proof as this truth has. If the early church always baptized in the name of Jesus, surely this is the correct and only way to be baptized today.

V. WATER BAPTISM IS PART OF THE GREAT COMMISSION

A. STATEMENT OF SCRIPTURE

1. "Go ye therefore, and teach all nations, baptizing them in the name of the Father, and of the Son, and of the Holy Ghost" (Matthew 28:19).

2. "Go ye into all the world, and preach the gospel to every creature. He that believeth and is baptized shall be saved" (Mark 16:15-16).

B. STATEMENT OF TRUTH

Since water baptism is part of the great commission, it is not left to our choice. Not only are we to be baptized ourselves, but we are to preach baptism as part of the gospel and to baptize converts when they have repented.

C. EXPOSITION OF TRUTH

The great commission is a command to the church, which was not to be questioned but to be obeyed fully. The Lord spoke this commission on at least three occasions to His disciples during the forty days between His resurrection and His ascension. It is recorded in all four Gospels and in the Acts of the Apostles. If Jesus repeated this commission at least three times, and each of the Gospels have so faithfully recorded it, we can readily understand that the importance of the commission is indeed great.

In the commission Jesus commanded His disciples to:

1. Go into all the world (Mark 16:15).
2. Preach the gospel to every creature (Mark 16:15).
3. Teach (make disciples of) all nations (Matthew 28:19).
4. Baptize them in the divine name (Matthew 28:19).
5. Teach observance of everything He had commanded (Matthew 28:19).

Along with going, preaching, teaching, we are commanded to baptize. Baptism is not something to be left to our own mood or desire, but the commission calls for explicit obedience. To obey this command it is necessary to baptize just as Jesus commanded us: "in the name." When a minister merely repeat the words "Father, Son, and Holy Ghost" in water baptism, he is not obeying the commission. In this case the minister is only repeating the words of Jesus and not obeying them. Obedience calls for water baptism in the name of Jesus.

D. APPLICATION OF TRUTH

Obedience to the great commission demands that each one of us be baptized into the name of Jesus, that we preach the gospel of the kingdom in all the world (Matthew 24:14), and that we baptize converts in the name of Jesus. It is also evident that the gospel of the kingdom includes the message of the name of Jesus (Luke 24:47).

VI. ALL ARGUMENTS AGAINST WATER BAPTISM IN JESUS' NAME ARE EASILY ANSWERED

A. STATEMENT OF SCRIPTURE

1. "And they continued stedfastly in the apostles' doctrine" (Acts 2:42).

2. "When they heard this, they were baptized in the name of the Lord Jesus" (Acts 19:5).

3. "But if we walk in the light, as he is in the light . . ." (I John 1:7).

4. "That ye should earnestly contend for the faith which was once delivered unto the saints" (Jude 3).

B. STATEMENT OF TRUTH

Many people bring arguments against the truth of water baptism in Jesus' name. However, we can easily answer all such arguments by the Word of God.

C. EXPOSITION OF TRUTH

The Scriptures give a strong foundation for the truth of water baptism in the name of Jesus Christ. Nevertheless, we shall deal with four arguments often brought against it. From our discussion, we will readily see that all such reasoning is without scriptural foundation.

1. "*We should accept the words of Jesus rather than Peter*." Anyone who makes this statement actually says

that there is a contradiction in the Bible. However, Matthew 28:19 and Acts 2:38 do not contradict one another. The words of the apostle Peter in Acts 2:38 tell us how we may obey Matthew 28:19. The name is singular. Father, Son, and Holy Ghost are titles, not names. What is the name? There can be but one answer: Jesus. Anyone who advances this argument is willing to repeat the words of Jesus but refuses to obey them.

2. "*Water baptism in Jesus' name is for the Jews only.*" Anyone who brings forth this argument actually says that there are two gospels: one for the Jews and one for the Gentiles. But there is only one gospel for both the Jew and the Gentile (Romans 1:16). Cornelius's household, the Ephesians, and the Corinthians were all Gentiles, and they were all baptized in Jesus' name. Jesus told us to preach the gospel in His name among all nations (Luke 24:47).

3. "*It makes no difference which way a person is baptized.*" If the formula is not important, then the mode of baptism is not important. Why not sprinkle, or pour, or immerse three times? If it makes no difference how we are baptized, then repentance will not make much difference, and it makes no difference whether or not a person speaks in tongues when he receives the Holy Ghost. All such reasoning is folly. If we are to be saved we must obey the gospel the Bible way. If a person is not baptized according to the Bible, he is not truly baptized.

4. "*We should never rebaptize, for there is only one baptism. It is quite sufficient if one was honest and sincere.*" The Ephesians were honest and sincere, yet they were rebaptized in the name of the Lord Jesus (Acts 19:5). It is true that there is only one baptism, but that is by immersion in the name of Jesus. Anyone who has not obeyed the Scriptures has not been baptized properly. Actually, then the term "rebaptize" is hardly correct, for a person is not truly baptized until he has been baptized in

the name of Jesus. Is a person honest and sincere who refuses to walk in the light of truth? All honest and sincere people will immediately desire to obey the Word of God when they see the truth.

D. APPLICATION OF TRUTH

Those who continue steadfastly in the apostles' doctrine and who contend for the faith need have no misgiving regarding their ability to defend the truth. All arguments against water baptism in Jesus' name are illogical, not scriptural, and easily refuted.

QUESTIONS

1. What is the meaning of the word *baptism*?
2. Explain the place that water baptism has in the plan of salvation.
3. What are the three elements that agree in the work of salvation?
4. What is the name of the Father, Son, and Holy Ghost?
5. Explain how water baptism is part of the great commission.
6. Name five things Jesus commanded us to do in the great commission.
7. On at least how many occasions did Jesus speak this commission?
8. What is the gospel of the kingdom?
9. Show the connection between repentance and water baptism.
10. Name five instances in the history of the early church where believers were baptized in the name of Jesus.

PROJECTS

1. Answer fully this argument against water baptism in the name of Jesus: "There were only Jews or Jewish proselytes at Pentecost. Therefore, Acts 2:38 is only for the Jews."

2. Using the text as a reference, write ten arguments in your own words in favor of water baptism in the name of Jesus.

NOTES

Chapter 6

Receiving The Holy Ghost (Resurrection)

I. BOTH TESTAMENTS PROMISE THE HOLY GHOST

A. STATEMENT OF SCRIPTURE

1. "And it shall come to pass afterward, that I will pour out my spirit upon all flesh; and your sons and your daughters shall prophesy, your old men shall dream dreams, your young men shall see visions" (Joel 2:28).

2. "For with stammering lips and another tongue will he speak to this people" (Isaiah 28:11).

3. "He shall baptize you with the Holy Ghost, and with fire" (Matthew 3:11).

4. "But the Comforter, which is the Holy Ghost, whom the Father will send in my name . . ." (John 14:26).

B. STATEMENT OF TRUTH

In the Old Testament both Joel and Isaiah prophesied about the baptism of the Holy Ghost. In the New Testament John the Baptist prophesied about, and Jesus promised, the Holy Ghost.

C. EXPOSITION OF TRUTH

We see the importance of the baptism of the Holy Ghost by two outstanding prophecies in the Old

Testament that foretold this experience. On the Day of Pentecost, when the crowd gathered, the apostle Peter clearly stated that this Pentecostal experience was what Joel had prophesied: "This is that which was spoken by the prophet Joel" (Acts 2:16). Isaiah's prophecy mentions stammering lips and another tongue. Paul applied his words to speaking in tongues by the power of the Spirit (I Corinthians 14:21-22).

John the Baptist clearly stated that Jesus Christ would baptize with the Holy Ghost and with fire. Jesus Himself gave His disciples the promise of the Holy Ghost (John 14:26; 15:26; 16:7). Jesus emphasized the importance of the Holy Ghost's coming by saying that it was necessary for Him to go away so that the Comforter might come. It was more important for the Comforter to come than for Jesus to remain in a physical body upon the earth. Not only did Jesus Christ promise the Holy Ghost to His disciples, He commanded them to remain in Jerusalem until the Holy Spirit came (Acts 1:4).

D. APPLICATION OF TRUTH

Not only do we have the promise that the Holy Ghost would come, but we have the historical record of the Comforter coming on the Day of Pentecost and of the apostolic church being baptized with the Holy Ghost. We also have the promise, given by the apostle Peter, that the Holy Ghost is for us today (Acts 2:39). We should not ask for any further testimony but simply believe the Word of God and receive.

E. DEFINITION OF TERM

Comforter: One who is called alongside to help, as a client calls a lawyer. The *Amplified Bible* gives the following synonyms to explain this term: Counselor, Helper, Intercessor, Advocate, Strengthener, and Standby.

II. THE HOLY GHOST WAS FIRST POURED OUT ON THE DAY OF PENTECOST

A. STATEMENT OF SCRIPTURE

1. "And when the day of Pentecost was fully come, they were all with one accord in one place. . . . And they were all filled with the Holy Ghost" (Acts 2:1, 4).

2. "But this is that which was spoken by the prophet Joel . . . I will pour out of my Spirit upon all flesh" (Acts 2:16-17).

B. STATEMENT OF TRUTH

The Holy Ghost was first poured out upon approximately 120 Jewish believers as they prayed in Jerusalem on the Day of Pentecost. This event was the birth of the New Testament church.

C. EXPOSITION OF TRUTH

1. *Before the Day of Pentecost.* To this time no one had been baptized with the Holy Ghost. The prophecies of the Old Testament and the promises of John the Baptist and our Lord all spoke of this glorious experience as being in the future. In the Old Testament the Holy Spirit rested upon holy people, and the prophets spoke as they were moved by the Holy Ghost (II Peter 1:21). However, not one of them had been baptized with the Holy Ghost. (See John 7:39; Hebrews 11:39.)

John the Baptist had been filled with the Holy Ghost from his mother's womb (Luke 1:15), and yet the Pentecostal experience was far more wonderful what he experienced (Matthew 11:11).

Jesus Christ said it was necessary for Him to go away so that the Comforter might come (John 16:7). This statement shows that it was not possible to receive the Comforter while Christ was here in the flesh. In fact, the Comforter is none other than the Spirit of Christ and could not be poured out until after Jesus had risen and ascended.

2. *Pentecost*. The Feast of Pentecost was one of the great pilgrimage feasts of Judaism, for which many of those who lived in remote sections of the Roman Empire returned to Jerusalem for worship. It was the culmination of the Feast of Weeks, at which were offered two loaves of bread representing the first products of the harvest. On this occasion, when Jews were gathered from all parts of the world, the Holy Ghost was poured out. As the Feast of Pentecost was the completion of the Feast of Weeks, so the outpouring of the Holy Ghost completed God's plan in providing salvation for humanity.

3. *Jesus commanded the disciples to tarry for the Holy Ghost.* That Jesus commanded his disciples to tarry in Jerusalem for the Holy Ghost reveals the importance of this Pentecostal experience (Luke 24:49; Acts 1:4). It is added proof that the Holy Ghost was not given until Pentecost (John 7:39).

4. *The birthday of the church*. The coming of the Comforter into the hearts of the approximately 120 believers was the beginning of the New Testament church. In the Gospels Jesus spoke of His church as still being future. "Upon this rock I will build my church" (Matthew 16:18). Clearly, the church had its beginning on this side of Calvary, on the Day of Pentecost. In fact, the church is a living organism indwelt by the Spirit and life of Jesus Christ. The Holy Ghost baptizes believers into the body of Christ so that members of the church are both filled with and baptized into the Spirit of Christ, which is the Holy Ghost (I Corinthians 12:13). Because of this, the church was born (brought into being) on the Day of Pentecost.

D. APPLICATION OF TRUTH

Since the Holy Ghost was poured out on the Day of

Pentecost and the church has not yet been raptured, the Holy Ghost is still here. Jesus commanded the disciples to tarry until Pentecost, but now it is only necessary to meet the terms of the gospel, which are (a) faith (John 7:38; Mark 16:17); (b) repentance (Acts 2:38); and (c) water baptism in the name of Jesus Christ for the remission of sins (Acts 2:38). If a person does not receive the Holy Ghost, it is evident that he has not met one of these conditions. It is possible for a person to receive the Spirit before water baptism if he has a willing and obedient heart (Acts 10:44-48).

E. DEFINITION OF TERM

1. *Pentecost*: A term meaning "fiftieth," which was applied to the fiftieth day after the Passover.

III. THE INITIAL EVIDENCE OF THE BAPTISM OF THE HOLY GHOST IS SPEAKING IN OTHER TONGUES

A. STATEMENT OF SCRIPTURE

1. "And they were filled with the Holy Ghost, and began to speak with other tongues, as the Spirit gave them utterance" (Acts 2:4).
2. "Which ye now see and hear" (Acts 2:33).
3. "For they heard them speak with tongues and magnify God" (Acts 10:46).
4. "And they spake with tongues, and prophesied" (Acts 19:6).

B. STATEMENT OF TRUTH

The evidence of the baptism of the Holy Ghost is that the newly Spirit-filled believer speaks in other tongues as the Spirit of God gives utterance. Some who has not spoken in tongues has not received the Holy Ghost according to the Scriptures.

C. EXPOSITION OF TRUTH

Many try to refute this truth and refuse to accept that the initial evidence of speaking in tongues always accompanies the baptism of the Holy Ghost. However, the testimony of the Scriptures is indisputable, giving conclusive proof that this supernatural manifestation always accompanies the Pentecostal experience. The record of the Scriptures is as follows:

1. *Prophesied.* In the Old Testament Isaiah prophesied of this manifestation. "For with stammering lips and another tongue will he speak to this people" (Isaiah 28:11). In the New Testament Jesus said tongues was one of the signs that would follow those who believe. "They shall speak with new tongues" (Mark 16:17).

2. *Experienced.* In every case except one, when the Bible records that men and women initially received the Holy Ghost in the New Testament church, it records that they spoke in tongues.

a. Jews on the Day of Pentecost (Acts 2:4).
b. Gentiles at Caesarea (Acts 10:46).
c. Ephesians (Acts 19:6).
d. Apostle Paul (I Corinthians 14:18).
e. Corinthians (I Corinthians 12:13; 14).

The only exception is in the eighth chapter of Acts, where we find the account of the Samaritans receiving the Holy Ghost (Acts 8:17). However, we should note that Simon the sorcerer offered money to buy the power of laying hands on believers that they might receive the Holy Spirit. It is evident that some supernatural manifestation accompanied the experience that the Samaritans received. If there had been no manifestation, Simon would never have been interested. On the Day of Pentecost there were both visible and audible manifestations. Undoubtedly Simon heard the audible manifestation of speaking in tongues. With such an overwhelming testimony of Scripture, who would dare seek to refute the truth that the baptism of the Holy Ghost is always accompanied with speaking in tongues? The apostle Paul said, "Forbid not to speak with tongues" (I Corinthians 14:39).

D. APPLICATION OF TRUTH

The only scriptural evidence we have that a person has been baptized with the Holy Ghost is that he speaks in tongues. If he has not spoken in tongues, then he has not received the Holy Spirit as the Scriptures teach, and he should seek God and pray until he does. A seeker should not pray for tongues but rather for the baptism of the Holy Ghost. The evidence of tongues will naturally be manifested when the Holy Ghost comes in.

IV. THE BAPTISM OF THE HOLY GHOST IS THE BIRTH OF THE SPIRIT

A. STATEMENT OF SCRIPTURE

1. "Except a man be born of water and of the Spirit, he cannot enter into the kingdom of God" (John 3:5).

2. "For by one Spirit are we all baptized into one body . . . and have been all made to drink into one Spirit" (I Corinthians 12:13).

3. "The Spirit itself beareth witness with our spirit, that we are the children of God" (Romans 8:16).

B. STATEMENT OF TRUTH

The baptism of the Holy Ghost is the birth of the Spirit in the experience of a believer.

C. EXPOSITION OF TRUTH

Jesus told Nicodemus that it was necessary to be born of water and of the Spirit in order for a person to enter the kingdom of God. A person experiences the birth of the Spirit when he is baptized with the Holy Ghost. We can best understand this truth when we compare the spiritual birth to the natural birth. As breath enters the lungs of the newborn babe and he cries out, even so the Holy Ghost enters the heart of the newborn child of God and he speaks in tongues.

Some people claim that the baptism of the Holy Ghost is not essential to salvation, saying it is only an endowment of power, an extra blessing that one may or may not receive. However, we may readily understand the place the baptism of the Holy Ghost has in God's plan of salvation if we consider the following facts:

1. Jesus never left it to the choice of His disciples; He *commanded* them to tarry until they received.

2. Jesus revealed how important it was for the Comforter to come when He said that it was expedient for Him to go away (John 16:7).

3. Only when a person has entered the kingdom of God and has been placed in the body of Christ can it be said that he is greater than John the Baptist (Matthew 11:11).

4. Jesus gave the apostle Peter the keys to the kingdom, and when he preached the gospel, thereby unlocking the door to the kingdom, he preached (a) repentance, (b) water baptism in Jesus' name, and (c) the baptism of the Holy Ghost (Acts 2:38). This alone is sufficient proof that the baptism of the Holy Ghost is the birth of the Spirit (John 3:5).

5. The apostle Paul wrote that we are saved "by the washing of regeneration, and renewing of the Holy Ghost" (Titus 3:5).

This truth completes a beautiful picture of full New Testament salvation and clearly explains such verses of Scripture as Romans 8:9 and Galatians 4:6, which emphasize the necessity of having the Spirit. Although we must understand the importance of the birth of the Spirit, we must also remember that the believer has already received much from God in repentance and water baptism in Jesus' name.

D. APPLICATION OF TRUTH

Every believer must seek God until he is baptized with the Holy Ghost and has entered the kingdom of God. At the same time, we should not discourage him by minimizing the experience he already has. He should be truly thankful for what he has already received from God and press on into the kingdom.

V. THE BAPTISM OF THE HOLY GHOST IDENTIFIES US WITH CHRIST IN RESURRECTION

A. STATEMENT OF SCRIPTURE

1. "We shall be also in the likeness of his resurrection" (Romans 6:5).

2. "If ye then be risen with Christ . . ." (Colossians 3:1).

3. "Even so in Christ shall all be made alive" (I Corinthians 15:22).

4. "But if the Spirit of him that raised up Jesus from the dead dwell in you, he . . . shall also quicken your mortal bodies by his Spirit that dwelleth in you" (Romans 8:11).

B. STATEMENT OF TRUTH

As Jesus experienced death, burial, and resurrection in providing salvation, we experience death, burial, and resurrection in receiving salvation. In the baptism of the Holy Ghost we experience resurrection.

C. EXPOSITION OF TRUTH

The new birth places us "in Christ." Only as we are members of His body can we have hope of the first resurrection and the rapture of the church (I Thessalonians 4:16). The baptism of the Holy Ghost places us in the body and gives us this hope (I Corinthians 12:13).

If we are to be in Christ, it is only reasonable to expect that in salvation the church will experience death, burial, and resurrection. We may state this process as follows: we experience (a) death in repentance, (b) burial in water baptism in Jesus' name, and (c) resurrection in the baptism of the Holy Ghost.

D. APPLICATION OF TRUTH

The Spirit-filled believer experiences a definite resurrection as he rises to walk in newness of life. He was dead (Ephesians 2:1), but now he lives. This experience gives the child of God hope in the physical resurrection at the coming of the Lord.

VI. THE HOLY GHOST IS THE SPIRIT OF CHRIST

A. STATEMENT OF SCRIPTURE

1. "Now the Lord is that Spirit" (II Corinthians 3:17).
2. "Now if any man have not the Spirit of Christ, he is none of his" (Romans 8:9).
3. "Which is Christ in you, the hope of glory" (Colossians 1:27).
4. "I will not leave you comfortless: I will come to you" (John 14:18).

B. STATEMENT OF TRUTH

There is only one Spirit, and in the baptism of the Holy Ghost we receive the Spirit of Christ.

C. EXPOSITION OF TRUTH

There is only one Spirit (Ephesians 4:4). If there were three persons in the Godhead, then it would be reasonable to conclude that there are three Spirits in the Godhead. It would also be reasonable to conclude that the Spirit-filled believer would receive three distinct Spirits, for Scripture states that he is filled with God

(Ephesians 3:19), with the Holy Ghost (Acts 2:4), and with Christ (Colossians 1:27). However, there is only one, undivided Godhead, and a believer is filled with only one Spirit. The Scriptures, experience, and logic all verify this fact.

Since there is only one Spirit, it only remains to identify that one Spirit. Again we find the Bible is quite specific on this point. "Now the Lord is that Spirit" (II Corinthians 3:17). What more do we need to understand that the Holy Ghost is the Spirit of Christ? When Jesus promised to send the Comforter, He said, "I will come to you." When a believer receives the Holy Spirit into his heart, it is none other than the Spirit of Christ who enters. By this means the prayer is answered:

> Into my heart, into my heart,
> Come into my heart, Lord Jesus.
> Come in today; come into stay;
> Come into my heart, Lord Jesus.

When a believer is baptized with the Holy Ghost, he is both baptized into Christ and filled with Christ. Of him we can say: (a) he is in Christ (I Corinthians 12:13) and (b) Christ is in him (Colossians 1:27). We may illustrate this truth by placing a drinking glass in a pail of water. The glass is in the water, and the water is in the glass. Likewise, we are in Christ, and Christ is in us.

D. APPLICATION OF TRUTH

This truth helps to make very clear just who is ready to be raptured when Jesus comes. What a glorious privilege it is to be "in Christ" and to have "Christ in us"!

QUESTIONS

1. What two Old Testament passage prophesy about the baptism of the Holy Ghost?

2. In the New Testament who prophesied of this experience?

3. What is the meaning of the word *Pentecost*?

4. When is the birthday of the church?

5. What is the initial evidence of the baptism of the Holy Ghost?

6. What did Simon the sorcerer desire to buy? Why?

7. Who is the Holy Spirit?

8. How many divine Spirits are there?

9. Why is the baptism of the Holy Ghost important?

10. Give two reasons why we know that Jesus considered it very important for us to receive the Holy Spirit.

PROJECTS

1. Do the necessary research and write a brief history of the Pentecostal church today.

2. Write a brief history of how the Pentecostal church started in your home town.

NOTES

Chapter 7
Holiness

I. GOD IS HOLY

A. STATEMENT OF SCRIPTURE

1. "And ye shall be holy unto me: for I the LORD am holy" (Leviticus 20:26).

2. "Because it is written, Be ye holy; for I am holy" (I Peter 1:16).

3. "God is light, and in him is no darkness at all" (I John 1:5).

B. STATEMENT OF TRUTH

God is absolutely perfect in true holiness. Only God is holy in Himself and possesses the attribute of true holiness.

C. EXPOSITION OF TRUTH

The holiness of God refers to His absolute moral purity. He can neither sin nor tolerate sin. God is absolutely perfect in righteousness, and in Him is not the slightest degree of imperfection or impurity.

The root meaning of the word *holy* is "separated." It means to withdraw from what is common or unclean and be consecrated to what is sacred and pure. In what sense is God separated? He is perfect; humans are imperfect. God is divine; humans are not. He is morally perfect, humans are sinful. As applied to God, the term *holiness* signifies His separation from and transcendence over all His creation.

Holiness is the attribute that God would have us remember about Him more than any other. The visions that God gave to Job, Moses, and Isaiah show this very definitely. Thirty times the prophet Isaiah spoke of God as the "Holy One." It is because of this attribute that God cannot have fellowship with sinners. God hates sin; to Him it is vile and detestable. There is an infinite distance between the sinner and God because of sin. The sinner and God are at opposite poles of the moral universe. Herein lies the need of atonement, which bridges this awful distance.

Only God is truly holy within Himself. He is the only source of absolute perfection and true holiness. Since there is only one God, there can only be one source of the sacred and divine.

D. APPLICATION OF TRUTH

It is evident that humans must become holy before they can have fellowship with a holy God. This condition of holiness comes only as people consecrate themselves to God and the presence of God comes into their lives. Another important application is that we have right views of sin when we have right views of the holiness of God.

E. DEFINITION OF TERMS

1. *Attribute*: A quality or characteristic, in this case belonging to God.

2. *Consecration*: An act involving both the divine and human. Our part is to separate ourselves from sin and dedicate ourselves to the service of God; God's part is to make us sacred and holy with His own presence.

II. HOLINESS IS ESSENTIAL TO SALVATION

A. STATEMENT OF SCRIPTURE

1. "Follow peace with all men, and holiness, without which no man shall see the Lord" (Hebrews 12:14).

2. "Blessed are the pure in heart: for they shall see God" (Matthew 5:8).

3. "A glorious church, not having spot, or wrinkle, or any such thing; but that it should be holy and without blemish" (Ephesians 5:27).

B. STATEMENT OF TRUTH

Only those who are holy and sanctified shall be able to see Jesus as their Lord and Savior and enter into His kingdom. Holiness is essential to salvation.

C. EXPOSITION OF TRUTH

We may readily understand the importance of holiness to salvation as we consider two basic facts:

1. *The nature of fellowship with God.* The sin of our first parents broke the fellowship between Jehovah and Adam and Eve. The presence of sin created an infinite gulf between the holy God and sinful humans. So long as sin exists, there can be no true fellowship. The sin question has to be dealt with and humans must sanctified before fellowship can be restored. Unless humans become holy there can be no fellowship. Salvation is actually the bestowal of eternal fellowship between God and humans. Therefore, there can be no salvation without humans acquiring holiness.

2. *The nature of our eternal home.* No sin shall enter heaven. "And there shall in no wise enter into it any thing that defileth, neither whatsoever worketh abomination, or maketh a lie" (Revelation 21:27). If sin could enter heaven, it would immediately cease to be heaven. Only the righteous, pure, and holy will have the right to enter the eternal home the Lord has prepared for His children. Heaven is a prepared place, prepared by a holy God for a holy people. Therefore, holiness is essential to salvation.

In his epistle to the Ephesian church, the apostle Paul wrote that the bride will be a glorious church without spot, wrinkle, or blemish. Without holiness no one can have the hope of being part of the church and ready for the Lord's return.

D. APPLICATION OF TRUTH

If an individual does not live a clean, pure, holy life, it is evident that he is not partaking of God's holiness. A person who lives in sin will never go to heaven if he dies in that condition without being born again. If a born-again person sins, he must confess that sin and repent of it so that he will receive forgiveness and continue to enjoy fellowship with God now and for eternity (I John 1:6-9). Whether or not a person is saved will be revealed by his life (Matthew 7:20).

E. DEFINITION OF TERM

Sanctify: To separate from evil and dedicate to the service of God. Whatever is devoted exclusively to the service of God is sanctified.

III. THE HOLY SPIRIT IMPARTS HOLINESS TO HUMANS

A. STATEMENT OF SCRIPTURE

1. "We . . . are changed into the same image from glory to glory, even as by the Spirit of the Lord" (II Corinthians 3:18).
2. "That he might sanctify and cleanse it with the washing of water by the word" (Ephesians 5:26).
3. "By the which will we are sanctified through the offering of the body of Jesus Christ once for all" (Hebrews 10:10).

B. STATEMENT OF TRUTH

The presence and power of the Holy Spirit in one's life make him holy. Each person has the responsibility to bring himself to the sanctifying influence of the Holy Spirit and allow God's will to be done.

C. EXPOSITION OF TRUTH

It is the presence of God in one's life that makes him holy. Fallen, sinful humans are wholly incapable of making themselves holy, for this attribute belongs solely to God. Just as it took the presence of God in the burning bush to make the sands of the wilderness "holy ground," even so it takes the presence of God in a person's life to make him holy.

Under both testaments, righteousness and holiness are reckoned to believers by the grace of God. Under the law, however, a person actually became righteous only by doing righteously to the best of his ability; under grace, he is able to do righteously because he has first been made righteous by the new birth. In the Old Testament, righteousness was imputed; in the New Testament church, righteousness is both imputed and imparted.

Apart from the presence and power of the Holy Spirit in his life, which causes him to become a new creation, a person can never become holy. He may be moral and upright in many ways, but he is still a sinner until he is born again and sanctified by the power of the Holy Ghost. Apart from God, all his righteousness is as filthy rags (Isaiah 64:6).

The work of sanctification begins in a person's life when he hears or reads the gospel message, for the Word of God has a cleansing influence in the heart of the hearer. "Now ye are clean through the word which I have spoken unto you" (John 15:3). "Sanctify them through thy truth: thy word is truth" (John 17:17). There is a definite power in God's Word to convict of sin and to exert a sanctifying influence in the life of a penitent.

Although the Holy Spirit accomplishes the work of sanctification, yet each person has a definite responsibility in becoming holy. As someone who is cold brings himself to the fire and is warmed, so an unholy person brings himself to Jesus and is made holy. It is his responsibility to bring himself to, and keep himself under, the sanctifying influence of God. He does so by repentance, surrender, consecration, dedication, separation from the world, faith, and obedience. In doing this, he does only only what is a reasonable and expected expression of faith; he does nothing that earns any merit or reward.

D. APPLICATION OF TRUTH

Although we cannot make ourselves holy apart from God, yet we have a definite responsibility in becoming holy, for God has provided the means by which we may be sanctified. If we refuse to surrender ourselves to the power of the Holy Spirit, we shall remain unsanctified and without excuse.

IV. SANCTIFICATION IS A CONTINUOUS WORK OF GRACE

A. STATEMENT OF SCRIPTURE

1. "But grow in grace, and in the knowledge of our Lord and Saviour Jesus Christ" (II Peter 3:18).

2. "Work out your own salvation with fear and trembling" (Philippians 2:12).

3. "We . . . are changed into the same image from glory to glory, even as by the Spirit of the Lord" (II Corinthians 3:18).

B. STATEMENT OF TRUTH

The work of sanctification is a continuous and progressive work of grace in the life of the child of God. So long as he remains in this life, there will be growth in spirituality and perfection. This occurs as he lives a Spirit-filled life.

C. EXPOSITION OF TRUTH

The exhortations of the apostle Peter to grow in grace and in the knowledge of Jesus Christ and of the apostle Paul to work out our own salvation with fear and trembling, prove that sanctification is a progressive work in our lives. Further exhortations are:

1. To perfect holiness in the fear of God (II Corinthians 7:1).

2. To increase and abound in love (I Thessalonians 3:12).

3. To increase more and more (I Thessalonians 4:10).

All of these exhortations show that sanctification is progressive and continues in the life of a saint until he leaves this life.

We may view sanctification in three tenses: past, present, and future. We may speak of sanctification as instantaneous, progressive, or complete. Sanctification begins with the hearing of the gospel message and continues through repentance, faith, and water baptism in the name of Jesus. However, the work of sanctification is chiefly accomplished through the baptism of the Holy Spirit. In the act of regeneration the life is sanctified and holiness is imparted by the presence and power of the Holy Spirit. In this sense we may consider sanctification as past tense and instantaneous.

Actually this is only the beginning of the work of sanctification, which continues on throughout this life. Growth in spirituality and maturity of holiness takes place as the result of a Spirit-filled life. The Christian who is filled with the Spirit (Ephesians 5:18), who walks after the Spirit (Romans 8:1-4), and who is led by the Spirit (Romans 8:14), lives a life of victory over sin, where there is no condemnation. In fact, the only way he can live above condemnation is to live the Spirit-filled life and to be led by the Spirit of God. In this sense, we may consider sanctification as present tense and progressive.

Finally, of course, the work of perfection will occur at the rapture of the church. In this sense, we may consider sanctification as future, and at that time it will be complete.

D. APPLICATION OF TRUTH

If someone finds it difficult to overcome a fault or sin in his life, the quickest way to victory is to seek a closer walk in the Holy Spirit. By being Spirit-filled and being led by the Holy Spirit, he will be able to overcome temptation and live above sin. Every Christian should be able to see a definite growth in spirituality and holiness.

V. THERE ARE TWO GENERAL ASPECTS OF PERFECTION

A. STATEMENT OF SCRIPTURE

1. "Let us go on unto perfection" (Hebrews 6:1).

2. "Not as though I had already attained, either were already perfect: but I follow after" (Philippians 3:12).

3. "Let us cleanse ourselves from all filthiness of the flesh and spirit, perfecting holiness in the fear of God" (II Corinthians 7:1).

B. STATEMENT OF TRUTH

We may consider perfection as either absolute or relative. We cannot improve upon what belongs to God, while we can always improve upon what belongs to humanity.

C. EXPOSITION OF TRUTH

1. *Absolute perfection.* No one can improve upon absolute perfection. In this sense there can be no degrees of perfection. This kind of perfection belongs only to God. He is perfect in every attribute, and in Him is not the slightest degree of imperfection. Not only is He perfect, but everything He does is perfect.

When God saves someone, that person is perfectly saved. A person is either saved or not saved. If he is born again, he cannot be more born again. His position or standing in Christ is perfect and cannot be improved upon. This is the work of the Holy Spirit in his life, and therefore it is perfect.

2. *Relative perfection.* Relative perfection fulfills the end for which it is designed. This is type of perfect is possible for humans to attain in this life. It describes what is actually wrought in the saint's character. It involves growth and maturity. A Christian may walk perfectly in all the light and knowledge that he has and yet in many ways still be imperfect. He may be blameless and yet at the same time not faultless.

We may illustrate this truth by considering a small infant creeping upon the floor. The parents undoubtedly look upon their child as perfect. However, if after two or three years that child still creeps and has not learned to walk, the parents would be deeply concerned and no longer would look upon their child as perfect. In grade one, a pupil might receive a perfect grade in a test in mathematics, but he certainly could not do so if handed a test for grade eight. It is possible for someone to be perfect in his studies but be just at the beginning of his studies.

Likewise, the child of God may be perfect in his walk with God but just at the beginning of his growth in spiritual knowledge and character. Holiness demands that he continue to walk in the light of the revealed will of God. If he does this, he achieves relative perfection in his life and is blameless. If he refuses and disobeys, he comes under condemnation, and unless he repents he will backslide and lose his soul.

D. APPLICATION OF TRUTH

It is the Christian's duty to strive after perfection

(Matthew 5:48). Every child of God is perfectly saved, and yet no one will reach a place of absolute perfection in his character and knowledge in this life. For this reason everyone should reach for perfection and should perfect holiness in the fear of God (II Corinthians 7:1).

A mature saint of God should be able to look back and see, by the grace of God, great growth and advancement in his spiritual life. At the same time, he should not judge a young convert by himself. Everyone should extend great patience and understanding to all babes in Christ.

VI. HOLINESS DEMANDS A PRACTICAL WALK OF OBEDIENCE TO THE WILL OF GOD

A. STATEMENT OF SCRIPTURE

1. "Not every one that saith unto me, Lord, Lord, shall enter into the kingdom of heaven; but he that doeth the will of my Father which is in heaven" (Matthew 7:21).

2. "And be not conformed to this world: but be ye transformed by the renewing of your mind, that ye may prove what is that good, and acceptable, and perfect, will of God" (Romans 12:2).

3. "Doing the will of God from the heart" (Ephesians 6:6).

4. "What manner of persons ought ye to be in all holy conversation and godliness" (II Peter 3:11).

B. STATEMENT OF TRUTH

The walk of holiness is a practical, down-to-earth experience of victorious living in obedience to the will of God. This every child of God can do.

C. EXPOSITION OF TRUTH

1. *A correct understanding of holiness is necessary.* Some people think of holiness as angelic, mystical,

and completely removed from this world. This is certainly not the case, for the walk of holiness is a practical, down-to-earth experience of victory. Holiness is revealed by every word, every step, every act conforming to God's revealed will. It is living outwardly the divine life of Jesus that dwells inwardly. If a person does not walk straight and live right, it is evident that his inward spiritual life is lacking.

2. *The will of God always is possible.* The revealed will of God always begins with the Word of God. God never asks someone to do anything that is contrary to His Word. If the Scriptures contain a command for us, then it is not necessary for us even to pray about whether we should do it. It simply calls for obedience, no more and no less. For example, it is not necessary to ask God whether or not one should be baptized in Jesus' name, attend church regularly, tithe, tell the truth, be honest in business dealings, dress modestly, and so on. The Word of God clearly states all these teachings, and we should explicitly obey them without hesitation.

God never asks a person to do something that is impossible for him to do. God's will is always possible. If it is the will of God, it can be done. God only holds people responsible for what they can do.

3. *Holiness affects every part of our lives.* No part of a person's life is unaffected by holiness. It is useless to argue that the heart can be holy while the outward person is worldly. It is impossible for someone to live this way. If the heart is holy, the outward person is going to conform. The condition of a person's heart is revealed by the way he lives, by the way he talks, dresses, and acts. The will of God influences his business dealings, his home relations, his reading habits, his dress, his conversation, and his spare time. If holiness is present in his life, he will endeavor to do God's will as it pertains to each moment of his day, each step of the way, and each phase of his life.

4. *A holy life is always possible.* Holiness is simply walking straight and doing what is right. By the grace of God everyone can do this. Holiness never requires someone to do what is impossible, such as playing an instrument in the orchestra when he has no talent for music. Holiness simply requires him to walk in the revealed will of God, one step at a time. This, everyone can do. Everyone can tell the truth, deal honestly, dress modestly, refrain from worldly and ungodly amusements, and so on. Every person can live a life of holiness. There is never any excuse for sin. If someone does not live holy, he is inexcusable.

5. *The rewards of holy living are many.* Holiness pays great dividends in this life as well as being essential to salvation. Here is a partial list of the blessings of holiness to the Christian:

a. He has greater peace of mind and heart.

b. He has far greater health and will live longer.

c. He enjoys greater happiness in his home if his family are all living for God.

d. He tends to be more prosperous in material things.

e. His life is more fruitful, for he lives a life of service to others.

Beside all this, a life of holiness by the grace of God means the salvation of the soul and meeting the Lord without condemnation.

6. *Some simple guidelines for a holy life.*

a. Receive the Holy Spirit in your life and live a Spirit-filled life.

b. Pray much. A prayerful life will usually be a holy life.

c. Read the Bible much and attend Bible studies. The Word of God will have a sanctifying influence in your life.

d. God's revealed will begins in His Word. Obey the Word of God without hesitation.

e. Dedicate yourself fully to His service and to His will.

f. Remember that you *can* live holy; a life of holiness is indeed possible.

g. Remember that you need claim the victory only one day at a time.

h. Keep your eyes off the faults of others and look to Jesus.

i. Keep your eyes off your own weakness and look to Jesus.

j. Testify and witness often and at every opportunity (Revelation 12:11).

k. Discuss your problems freely with your pastor.

l. When in doubt concerning a certain practice, ask the following: (1) Does the Bible condemn this? (2) Can I pray and ask Jesus to bless it? (3) Can I take Jesus with me while practicing it? (4) Will this be a blessing to others? (5) Will this be a stumbling stone to anyone? (6) Will this hinder, in any manner, my service to Jesus?

D. APPLICATION OF TRUTH

This truth gives a person great confidence. When we understand that we *can* live holy lives by the help of the Lord, generally the battle is won and we have the victory.

E. PRACTICAL APPLICATION OF HOLINESS

Following is some important practical instruction on holiness from the Articles of Faith of the United Pentecostal Church International:

> Godly living should characterize the life of every child of the Lord, and we should live according to the pattern and example given in the Word of God. "For the grace of God that bringeth salvation hath appeared to all men, teaching us that, denying ungodliness and worldly lusts, we should live soberly, righteously, and godly, in this present world" (Titus 2:11-12). "For even hereunto were ye called: because Christ also suffered

for us, leaving us an example, that ye should follow his steps: who did no sin, neither was guile found in his mouth: who, when he was reviled, reviled not again; when he suffered, he threatened not; but committed himself to him that judgeth righteously" (I Peter 2:21-23).

"Follow peace with all men, and holiness, without which no man shall see the Lord" (Hebrews 12:14).

"But as he which hath called you is holy, so be ye holy in all manner of conversation; because it is written, Be ye holy; for I am holy. And if ye call on the Father, who without respect of persons judgeth according to every man's work, pass the time of your sojourning here in fear: forasmuch as ye know that ye were not redeemed with corruptible things, as silver and gold, from your vain conversation received by tradition from your fathers; but with the precious blood of Christ, as of a lamb without blemish and without spot" (I Peter 1:15-19).

We wholeheartedly disapprove of our people indulging in any activities which are not conducive to good Christianity and godly living, such as theaters, dances, mixed bathing or swimming, women cutting their hair, makeup, any apparel that immodestly exposes the body, all worldly sports and amusements, and unwholesome radio programs and music. Furthermore, because of the display of all these evils on television, we disapprove of any of our people having television sets in their homes. We admonish all of our people to refrain from any of these practices in the interest of spiritual progress and the soon coming of the Lord for His church.

QUESTIONS

1. How does someone become holy?
2. Explain how holiness is essential to salvation.

3. Explain fully the term "relative perfection."

4. How is sanctification an instantaneous work of grace in a person's life?

5. How is sanctification a progressive work in a person's life?

6. What is the connection between a life of holiness and the will of God?

7. What is the connection between a life of holiness and the Bible?

8. What rewards does a holy life have in this world?

9. What is the connection between a person's heart and his everyday walk?

10. What instructions would you give a young convert on how to begin living a victorious life?

PROJECTS

1. Write a paper of at least three hundred words on the following statement: "It pays to live a holy life."

2. Copy the guidelines given in the text for living a holy life. Think of several more guidelines of your own, and add to this list.

NOTES

Chapter 8
Divine Healing

I. THE BIBLE TEACHES DIVINE HEALING FOR OUR BODIES

A. STATEMENT OF SCRIPTURE

1. "For I am the LORD that healeth thee" (Exodus 15:26).

2. "And with his stripes we are healed" (Isaiah 53:5).

3. "They shall lay hands on the sick, and they shall recover" (Mark 16:18).

4. "And the prayer of faith shall save the sick" (James 5:15).

B. STATEMENT OF TRUTH

The Bible clearly teaches that there is divine healing for our bodies; divine healing is a definite doctrine of the Scriptures.

C. EXPOSITION OF TRUTH

As faith is possibly the most important element in receiving healing for our bodies, it is necessary to establish firmly the scriptural foundation for this truth. Faith must ever rest on the Word of God. One cannot pray the "prayer of faith" until he is fully persuaded that divine healing is part of the gospel.

It is easy to establish the scriptural foundation for this

truth, for the message continues throughout the pages of the Bible.

1. *Promise to the Israelites* (Exodus 15:25-26). Immediately after the crossing of the Red Sea the Lord gave to the Israelites a promise of healing. This took place right at the beginning of their journey in the wilderness, letting them know that sickness belonged to the old life of bondage in Egypt. This was not only a promise, but it was also a statute and an ordinance. Likewise Jesus would have us understand at the very beginning of our pilgrimage that sickness belongs to the old life and that He has left for us a distinct ordinance of healing in His name (James 5:14).

2. *The exhortation of David* (Psalm 103:3). David exhorted us to not forget all the benefits of the Lord. He gave God the glory for the salvation of the soul and healing of the body. The same verse joins both benefits, showing that there is a definite connection between these two blessings.

3. *Isaiah's prophecy* (Isaiah 53:5). The prophet pictured Jesus Christ not only as our sin bearer but also as the One who has carried our sicknesses and our pains. This verse of Scripture shows Jesus Christ to be the Great Physician as well as the sacrificial Lamb upon the cross.

4. *The great commission* (Mark 16:17-18). In this passage of Scripture one of the signs that shall follow the preaching of the gospel is that the sick will be healed. In fact, we may conclude that divine healing is part of the gospel itself.

5. *The gifts of the Spirit* (I Corinthians 12:8-10). The indwelling presence of the Holy Ghost imparts supernatural gifts of the Spirit to the New Testament church. One of these nine gifts is "the gifts of healing."

6. *The instruction of James* (James 5:13-15). This instruction of James to the church is actually a command to obey. It shows us God's method of dealing with sickness.

7. *Jesus Christ is, ever the same* (Hebrews 13:8).

The unchanging character of Jesus Christ is one of the greatest proofs we need that He heals today. During His ministry upon earth Jesus healed all who were brought to Him (Matthew 8:16). If He bore our pains in His own body on the cross, surely He will do for His children today what He did when He was here upon earth.

To the above verses of Scripture we may add all the passages of Scripture that relate healings in both the Old and New Testaments.

D. APPLICATION OF TRUTH

Since we have believed for the salvation of our souls, we should also believe for healing of our bodies. The Bible provides such a strong foundation for the message of divine healing that everyone should readily believe Jesus is still the Great Physician.

II. THE ATONEMENT HAS PROVIDED HEALING FOR OUR BODIES

A. STATEMENT OF SCRIPTURE

1. "Who forgiveth all thine iniquities; who healeth all thy diseases" (Psalm 103:3).

2. "But he was wounded for our transgressions, he was bruised for our iniquities: the chastisement of our peace was upon him; and with his stripes we are healed" (Isaiah 53:5).

3. "Himself took our infirmities, and bare our sickness" (Matthew 8:17).

B. STATEMENT OF TRUTH

In the Atonement Jesus paid the price for the healing of our bodies as well as for the salvation of our souls.

C. EXPOSITION OF TRUTH

When Jesus took away our sins He removed the primary

cause for sickness from us. Although there are many secondary causes for sickness, we should always keep clearly in mind just what the primary cause of sickness really is. In the beginning God created Adam and Eve in perfect health. Sickness and death were unknown, and obedience to God's commands would have insured the permanence of this blessed condition. As a result of disobedience death came to the human race and with it sickness. Here we see the original cause of sickness.

When Jesus died, He bore not only our iniquities but also our sicknesses. In the Atonement is salvation for the soul and healing for the body. We see a beautiful type of this at Marah (Exodus 15:23-26). The tree that was cast into the bitter waters is a type of the cross of Calvary. The bitter waters are a type of sin. With the sweetening of the waters came a promise of health and healing.

D. APPLICATION OF TRUTH

It should be no more difficult to believe God for physical healing than for spiritual salvation. The need for each goes back to the same primary cause, and God's Word gives a solid foundation for believing for both of them. Actually, salvation is a greater miracle than healing.

III. DIVINE HEALING IS PROVIDED FOR EVERYONE

A. STATEMENT OF SCRIPTURE

1. "He cast out the spirits with his word, and healed all that were sick" (Matthew 8:16).

2. "There came also a multitude out of the cities round about unto Jerusalem, bringing sick folks, and them which were vexed with unclean spirits: and they were healed every one" (Acts 5:16).

3. "Is any among you afflicted? . . . Is any sick among you?" (James 5:13-14).

B. STATEMENT OF TRUTH

Even as God has provided salvation for the human race, so He has provided divine healing for the human race.

C. EXPOSITION OF TRUTH

When Jesus died upon the cross He died for the sins of the whole world. Jesus is no respecter of persons and shows no partiality when He offers eternal life to the sinner. Any individual in the whole world may meet the conditions of the gospel, come to Jesus, and be saved. Likewise, the Lord offers divine healing without showing partiality. He has provided healing for those who meet the conditions.

In His earthly ministry Jesus healed everyone who came or was brought to Him (Matthew 8:16). No case was too difficult for Him to heal. Jesus healed all manner of diseases including lunacy, epilepsy, leprosy, paralysis, fever, blindness, lameness, deafness, withered limbs, a sword cut, and so on. Jesus has not changed and is still able to heal all who come to Him.

This ministry of healing Jesus committed and transmitted to His church. In Acts 5:16 we read that they were healed every one. In the instructions of James to the church he asked, "Is any sick among you?" These passages of Scripture clearly show that healing is provided in the church for all.

D. APPLICATION OF TRUTH

Just as it is necessary to understand the terms of the gospel in order to meet its conditions, even so a person should study carefully the conditions attached to physical healing, knowing that God has provided both salvation and healing for all.

IV. OBJECTIONS TO DIVINE HEALING ARE EASILY ANSWERED

A. STATEMENT OF SCRIPTURE

1. "And they continued stedfastly in the apostles' doctrine and fellowship" (Acts 2:42).

2. "Jesus Christ the same yesterday, and to day, and for ever" (Hebrews 13:8).

3. "That ye should earnestly contend for the faith which was once delivered unto the saints" (Jude 3).

B. STATEMENT OF TRUTH

All popular objections to the ministry of divine healing are readily answered by the Word of God.

C. EXPOSITION OF TRUTH

Many objections have been raised against the gospel and ministry of physical healing. However, none of these objections is based upon a sound interpretation of the Scriptures, and as a rule, they are easily answered. We can answer many arguments against this wonderful truth by one verse of Scripture: "Jesus Christ the same yesterday, and to day, and for ever" (Hebrews 13:8).

It is impossible to prepare a complete list of arguments and objections against divine healing. We shall name only a few of the more common ones, so that one may readily see the unsound logic of all such reasoning.

1. "*The age of miracles is past.*" To this we might ask, "What age do we live in?" This is still the church age and will be until Jesus comes. The church age came into being with signs following (Acts 2:43). Jesus has not changed, the gospel has not changed, we are still in the church age, and therefore, the age of miracles is *not* past.

2. "*Miracles were needed to establish the church, but we do not need miracles today.*" Actually there is more unbelief and agnosticism in the world today than at

any period in human history. If there was ever a time when the church needed to have "signs following" and to reveal to a lost world a living Christ, it is today. The work of evangelism still continues, and people today need to see a Christ who hears and answers prayers.

3. "*False religions, and often wicked people, claim to have healings.*" Instead of proving that divine healing is wrong, this arguments shows that it is real. The devil will only imitate and counterfeit what is genuine. The Egyptian magicians were able to imitate the power of God by turning their rods into serpents. That the devil imitates the ministry of healing reveals that there is a real healing that comes from the Lord. How important it is for the church be able to present the true, real power of God.

4. "*It is presumptuous to pray to be healed; we should only pray for God's will.*" God has revealed His will in His Word. If it is in the Bible, we know it is His will. We actually insult Him if we reject when He already has revealed His will to us in His Word. Would Christ have borne our sickness at Calvary if it were not His will to heal? Would He have given us clear instructions on praying for the sick if it were not His will? He who healed multitudes during His earthly ministry will still heal people today.

5. "*God's only method of healing today is through medical science, which He has given us.*" It would certainly be wrong to discount what medical science is doing. The medical profession undoubtedly does much to relieve the sufferings of humanity. However, doctors work on a natural level, whereas God works on a spiritual level. Divine healing occurs on a higher level than medical science. The Creator always makes the correct diagnosis, He never makes a mistake, and when He heals, He heals completely.

There are many more arguments against the ministry of healing, but like those already mentioned, we may readily answer all of them by the Word of God.

D. APPLICATION OF TRUTH

If our faith is firmly grounded in the Word of God and we always remember that Jesus Christ does not change, no objection to the truth of divine healing will be able to affect our faith.

V. FAITH AND OBEDIENCE ARE ESSENTIAL TO BEING HEALED

A. STATEMENT OF SCRIPTURE

1. "What things soever ye desire, when ye pray, believe that ye receive them, and ye shall have them" (Mark 11:24).

2. "Not discerning the Lord's body. For this cause many are weak and sickly among you, and many sleep" (I Corinthians 11:29-30).

3. "Is any sick among you? let him call for the elders of the church; and let them pray over him, anointing him with oil in the name of the Lord" (James 5:14).

B. STATEMENT OF TRUTH

One must believe and obey the conditions set forth in God's Word in order to receive healing.

C. EXPOSITION OF TRUTH

Many promises of God are conditional. Just as the sinner who comes to the Lord for salvation must meet certain conditions before he is saved, a sick person must meet the conditions before he receives healing. Let us consider briefly these conditions under three headings.

1. *Removal of all hindrances*. There are many things in the life of an individual that may hinder him from being healed. Here is a partial list of such hindrances.

a. *Unconfessed sin* in the life of a person may hinder healing. In the Epistle of James we read that we are to confess our faults that we may be healed (James 5:16).

When we understand the close connection between salvation and healing as provided in the Atonement, we can readily see that unconfessed sin can hinder a person from being healed.

b. *An unforgiving spirit* is another great hindrance to healing. In fact, this may hinder any of our prayers from being answered. Jesus told us to forgive when we pray (Mark 11:25).

c. Sometimes, prayers are not answered because of wrong motives and desires. James said that we ask and do not receive because we ask amiss (James 4:3). We may state this hindrance as a *selfish and carnal spirit*.

d. The Bible directly connects a lack of healing with the *lack of discernment of the Lord's body* (I Corinthians 11:29). This refers to a lack of understanding of and faith in the sufferings and death of our Lord; unworthy participation in the ordinance of the Lord's Supper; and a lack of discernment of the Lord's mystical body on earth—the church.

e. Finally, we should mention the *lack of recognition of health rules*. The Lord created our bodies, and if we either ignorantly or willfully break the laws of health, we cannot have much faith for healing. Late hours, wrong diet, eating before retiring, and worry are some common ways in which the people of God can break health rules. These, along with the unclean habits of the sinner—such as drinking and smoking—may hinder healing.

2. *Obedience to the Word of God*. The Bible plainly states certain steps that a sick person may take in order to receive healing. Before he can expect to be healed he should obey them.

a. *Pray* (James 5:13). Prayer is essential in receiving from God and having our needs met. (See Luke 11:1-13.)

b. *Call for the elders of the church* (James 5:14). This certainly means the elders in one's own local assembly: the pastor and those who assist him in the ministry.

God will honor the pastor's prayers, for this is His instruction.

c. *Be anointed with oil in the name of the Lord* (James 5:14). The elders who pray exercise this ministry. Oil is a symbol of the Holy Spirit. The anointing takes place in the name of Jesus, for He is the Great Physician and the One who heals. There is healing in the name of Jesus (Acts 4:16).

d. *Have hands laid on* (Mark 16:18). Again this is the ministry of the elders who pray. The laying on of hands is also among the signs that follow those who believe. God honors the ministry of the laying on of hands, and through this act there is a definite impartation of the power of God.

3. *Faith.* Faith is essential for both salvation and healing. Without faith it is impossible to please God. All things are possible if we only believe. Faith is the hand that reaches out to receive from the Lord what we need.

The Lord not only honors the faith of the sick person but also the faith of the elders who pray. It is the "prayer of faith" that will save the sick (James 5:15). When Jesus saw the faith of the four men who brought the one sick of the palsy, He both forgave his sins and healed him (Mark 2:5). Certainly it is faith that the Lord honors, but in the case of healing, others may believe for the person who is ill. It is possible that a sick person might be too ill to exercise faith for himself.

VI. IT IS JESUS WHO HEALS

A. STATEMENT OF SCRIPTURE

1. "And his name through faith in his name hath made this man strong whom ye see and know" (Acts 3:16).

2. "By the name of Jesus Christ . . . even by him doth this man stand here before you whole" (Acts 4:10).

B. STATEMENT OF TRUTH

Humans cannot heal; Jesus Christ is the only One who can heal.

C. EXPOSITION OF TRUTH

When healings take place, it is Jesus Christ who does the healing. No mortal has the power to heal the body or to give life, for this prerogative belongs solely to God. Even physicians cannot heal; they bring about conditions that assist nature, but if healing takes place, it ultimately comes from the God who created the natural order. If this is true in medical science, it most certainly is true in the ministry of divine healing.

There is no such person as a "divine healer." Divine healing is genuine and real, but "divine healers" are fakes. True, there is the ministry of healing, and one of the nine listed gifts of the Spirit is "the gifts of healing." However, God has placed this ministry and this gift in the body, the Spirit-filled church. There is only One who may receive the glory, and He is the Great Physician, our Lord Jesus Christ.

Since Jesus is the healer, we readily see the importance of following closely the instructions of our Lord in His Word. Thus a sick person should call for his pastor to anoint and lay hands on him in the name of Jesus. The Lord will honor faith and obedience and will heal. Only Jesus Christ has the power to heal.

D. APPLICATION OF TRUTH

Possibly the main application here is to recognize that if Jesus is the One who heals, then one had better obey Him by calling for the elders of the church where the individual worships. It is a waste of time, effort, and money to drive hundreds of miles simply to be prayed for by some famous professed healer. It is the pastor's prayers that God will honor, for seeking prayer from the elders of the church is obedience to His Word.

QUESTIONS

1. What is the primary, original cause of sickness?
2. Give a type in the Old Testament of the double healing of body and soul.
3. For whom is healing of the body provided?
4. State two common objections to divine healing, and give the proper answer to each of these objections.
5. State two common hindrances to divine healing.
6. What instructions would you give to someone seeking for healing?
7. Who is the only divine healer?
8. Why is faith essential in receiving healing?
9. Why is obedience essential in receiving healing?

PROJECTS

1. Interview someone who has been healed by the Lord, and write out fully his testimonial.
2. Make a list of ten people in the Bible who were healed, and write briefly a description of the circumstances under which they were healed.

NOTES

Chapter 9

Gifts of The Spirit

I. THE CHURCH IS A SPIRIT-FILLED BODY

A. STATEMENT OF SCRIPTURE

1. "Know ye not that ye are the temple of God, and that the Spirit of God dwelleth in you?" (I Corinthians 3:16).

2. "For by one Spirit are we all baptized into one body, whether we be Jews or Gentiles, whether we be bond or free; and have been all made to drink into one Spirit" (I Corinthians 12:13).

3. "To the church, which is his body, the fulness of him that filleth all in all" (Ephesians 1:22-23).

B. STATEMENT OF TRUTH

The church is the mystical body of Christ, a living organism that the Holy Spirit dwells in and fills. As such, she is a spiritual body, and her life and ministry depend directly upon the power of the Holy Spirit within her.

C. EXPOSITION OF TRUTH

The New Testament church was born (brought into being) on the Day of Pentecost (Acts 2). At this time a spiritual organism was set up. The believers were baptized into the body, and Jesus Christ, in the Spirit, came to occupy His temple. This was the founding of the church.

The church is a living organism, not an organization. There is a vital relationship between Christ and the church, just as there is between the physical head and the body. We cannot join the church as we could join a lodge or any human organization. We must be partakers of Christ's life before we can become members of His church. The human body is one, yet it is made up of millions of living cells; in like manner, the body of Christ is one, though composed of millions of born-again souls. As the human body is vitalized by the soul, so the body of Christ is vitalized by the Holy Spirit. Pulsating through the veins and arteries of the church is the very life and presence of Jesus.

The Holy Spirit not only dwells in the child of God but also places him into the body of Christ (the church). It can now be said that he is "in Christ" (I Corinthians 15:22; I Thessalonians 4:16), and also Christ is in him (Colossians 1:27). We may illustrate this point by placing an empty cup into a pail of water. The cup is in the water, and the water is in the cup.

It is important that we clearly understand the work and ministry of the Holy Spirit for the church and in the church. First of all, salvation is the work of the Spirit. The Holy Ghost:

a. Convicts the sinner (John 16:8-13).

b. Regenerates the penitent (Titus 3:5).

c. Dwells in the child of God (Romans 8:9).

d. Baptizes into the body of Christ (I Corinthians 12:13).

e. Seals (Ephesians 1:13).

The Holy Ghost endows with power (Acts 1:8) and guides and teaches the child of God (John 16:13). The Christian is to walk after the Spirit (Romans 8:1)—to live and walk in the Spirit (Galatians 5:25).

By understanding the place that the Holy Spirit has in the church, we can readily see how that the work and ministry of the church depend directly upon the power and presence of the Holy Spirit dwelling within her. To provide for this, the Holy Spirit bears fruit in the life of every individual member and imparts spiritual gifts to the entire body.

D. APPLICATION OF TRUTH

How important it is that each member of the church remain Spirit-filled! Only when the church is Spirit-filled and fully yielded to the Holy Spirit can the church be healthy and growing. The church will then be able to maintain the unity of the Spirit and increase. The church will then bear the fruit of the Spirit and have the ministry of the gifts of the Spirit in her midst.

II. THERE ARE NINE FRUIT OF THE SPIRIT

A. STATEMENT OF SCRIPTURE

"But the fruit of the Spirit is love, joy, peace, longsuffering, gentleness, goodness, faith, meekness, temperance: against such there is no law" (Galatians 5:22-23).

B. STATEMENT OF TRUTH

There are nine fruit of the Spirit, which the Holy Spirit bears in the life of every Spirit-filled child of God.

C. EXPOSITION OF TRUTH

Although the word is a collective noun, in Galatians 5:22 "fruit" is in the singular. There are not nine separate fruits but rather one fruit. Even as a bunch of grapes is one cluster, so this cluster of graces is one fruit. If the Spirit bears one of these graces in the life of a Christian, the other eight graces may all be borne.

This is not the fruit of the Christian, but the fruit of the Holy Spirit. The Christian does not bear this fruit by his own power, but rather the Spirit bears the fruit in the life of the Christian.

Jesus referred to the Christian's fruit in John 15:8. The "much fruit" there is soul winning, and that is the fruit of the Christian.

Although there is one beautiful cluster of graces, nine graces are mentioned.

1. *Love* here is the "love of God . . . shed abroad in our hearts by the Holy Ghost" (Romans 5:5). It is both a love towards God and a love towards our fellow man. When we are injured or persecuted by someone, the Spirit will bear the fruit of love for that person.

2. *Joy* is not a happiness that results from having no troubles but a divine grace borne during times of distress, heaviness, and sorrow.

3. *Peace* is not the absence of tribulation but a quiet trust and confidence in God in the midst of trial and tribulation. Worry and anxiety go when the Holy Spirit bears the fruit of peace.

4. *Longsuffering* is patience and forbearance under adverse circumstances.

5. *Gentleness* is a kindly disposition, even while suffering; kindness.

6. *Goodness*. This word may be translated as "benevolence."

7. *Faith*. The meaning here is faithfulness, rather than belief.

8. *Meekness* does not mean servility, but rather true humility, submission to God's will, consideration for others.

9. *Temperance* is self-control and self-restraint, not only in regard to alcoholic beverages but mastery over all one's desires.

D. APPLICATION OF TRUTH

The Christian cannot bear these graces in his own natural ability. They can only be borne in the life of a Christian as he yields himself to God and permits the

Holy Spirit to bear the fruit. One must always remember that they are the fruit of the Spirit. If the Holy Spirit is there to bear one of these fruit, He will also bear the other eight in the life of the Spirit-filled child of God.

III. THERE ARE NINE GIFTS OF THE SPIRIT

A. STATEMENT OF SCRIPTURE

"For to one is given by the Spirit the word of wisdom; to another the word of knowledge by the same Spirit; to another faith by the same Spirit; to another the gifts of healing by the same Spirit; to another the working of miracles; to another prophecy; to another discerning of spirits; to another divers kinds of tongues; to another the interpretation of tongues" (I Corinthians 12:8-10).

B. STATEMENT OF TRUTH

There are nine gifts of the Spirit that the Holy Ghost has placed in the church but that are distributed to various members in the church. God has given these gifts for the benefit of the entire body.

C. EXPOSITION OF TRUTH

The nine gifts of the Spirit are in the church simply because of the presence of the Holy Ghost. Because they are gifts of the Spirit, they will be found wherever there is a Spirit-filled church. However, unlike the fruit of the Spirit, the gifts are diverse and distributed to everyone individually as the Lord wills (I Corinthians 12:11). There is one body and one Spirit, but the members are placed in the body according to the will of the Lord. Likewise the gifts of the Spirit are distributed within the body according to the Lord's will. The gifts are as follows:

1. *Word of wisdom.* This is not simply wisdom, but the *word* of wisdom. We see an example in the ministry of our Lord. The Pharisees tried to catch Jesus in His

words. His answer confounded them because it was the word of wisdom (Mark 12:14-17). He promised His disciples similar aid (Matthew 10:19-20).

2. *Word of knowledge.* Again we should note that this is not simply knowledge, but the *word* of knowledge. We see an example in the ministry of the apostle Paul, when he gave information on the outcome of the shipwreck in the storm (Acts 27:22-26).

3. *Faith.* The gift of faith by the Spirit does not make up for lack of faith or weak faith. It does not take the place of individual faith or saving faith, although even that is a gift of God (Ephesians 2:8). This gift of faith is a supernatural endowment by the Spirit, by which some special work is wrought through answered prayer. It is a special endowment of faith to meet a special need that arises in a church.

4. *Gifts of healing.* We see the importance of this gift by noting that it is mentioned two times near the close of the chapter (verses 28 and 30). We should also note that this gift is in the plural, *gifts* of healing, and in verse 28 both words are pluralized: "gifts of healings."

The reason for the plural is probably because of the many causes of sickness. Some ailments are caused by demon activity, through oppression, obsession, or possession. A sickness may be organic, and then again it may call for a correction of living habits before the Lord will heal. The human body is extremely complex, and there may be hundreds of reasons for sickness, both spiritual and physical. For this reason, the Spirit grants *gifts* of *healings*. We should also remember that every individual healing is a gift and should be received as such. For this reason also the gift would be in the plural.

Healing for our bodies is provided for in the Atonement. The Bible gives us definite instruction about the manifestation of this gift. It is not a human gift but rather the gift of the Holy Spirit, and if we obey God's

Word by calling for the elders (our pastors) we may see the gift in every local assembly.

5. *Working of miracles.* A miracle is a supernatural act on the natural plane. It is an act of God that to the natural person seems impossible and has no natural explanation. This gift is not for the purpose of display but rather to meet needs that arise in the protection and preservation of God's people (Mark 16:18; Acts 28:3-6).

6. *Prophecy.* New Testament prophecy is a *forth-telling* of scriptural truths; it is kept strictly within the framework of the Bible. Prophecy is speaking by inspiration in one's own mother tongue. Good, sound Spirit-anointed preaching becomes New Testament prophecy, along with anointed testimony from the laity (Revelation 19:10). Prophecy speaks to people for edification, exhortation, and comfort (I Corinthians 14:3).

7. *Discerning of spirits.* Satan has an army of demons always on the alert to disorganize the church and the individual Christian. To offset this work, the Holy Spirit gives to the body the discerning of spirits, making us aware of a wrong spirit and giving us knowledge of how to deal with these powers. It would seem that every successful pastor must have this gift, at least in a measure. It is one of the most important gifts for the church.

8. *Divers kinds of tongues.* In Scripture we find three different uses of speaking in other tongues:

a. When someone is baptized with the Holy Ghost (Acts 2:4).

b. Speaking to God in worship or prayer (I Corinthians 14:2, 14-15).

c. Addressing the church, coupled with interpretation (I Corinthians 14:13-27).

When speaking in tongues is used to address the church, it should operate in strict connection with interpretation (I Corinthians 14:27-28), and the combination of the two is similar to the gift of prophecy. It is a message addressed to the church, strictly in harmony with Bible truths.

9. *Interpretation of tongues.* The Christian who exercises this gift does not understand the language of the tongue he interprets. In the original, the word "interpret" does not mean to translate but to explain. The one who receives this gift explains the meaning of the message in tongues, yielding to the Spirit in giving forth the message.

D. APPLICATION OF TRUTH

In every Pentecostal assembly we may expect the Holy Spirit to manifest any one or more of the above gifts as the need arises. These are gifts of the Spirit, and if the Holy Spirit dwells in the church, we may be assured that the gifts will be manifested when needed.

IV. BOTH THE FRUIT AND THE GIFTS ARE MANIFESTED WHEN NEEDED

A. STATEMENT OF SCRIPTURE

1. "But the manifestation of the Spirit is given to every man to profit withal" (I Corinthians 12:7).

2. "Even so ye, forasmuch as ye are zealous of spiritual gifts, seek that ye may excel to the edifying of the church" (I Corinthians 14:12).

B. STATEMENT OF TRUTH

The fruit and the gifts of the Spirit are borne and manifested to meet definite needs that arise in the life of a church or individual.

C. EXPOSITION OF TRUTH

The Holy Spirit in the heart of the Christian is there to do a definite work, to meet a definite need. Although the fruit of the Spirit adorns the life of a saint, the fruit is not there just for show. Although the fruit of the Spirit brings enjoyment to the heart of the saint, the fruit is not just a toy to play with and to enjoy. When a definite need arises, the Holy Spirit will faithfully bear the fruit to meet that need. When someone has harmed us, for example, the Holy Spirit will bear the fruit of love for that person. When there is sorrow and distress, the Holy Spirit will bear the fruit of joy and peace. It is folly to try to display the fruit when there is no need, but when the need arises the Holy Spirit will bear the fruit. Because it is the fruit of the Spirit, all nine graces may be borne as the need arises.

The same principle holds true for the spiritual gifts. The gifts of the Spirit are not for display, to play with, to show off, or to prove the spirituality of a saint. They are in the body to meet the need of the body when that need arises. When the church needs to be comforted, edified, or exhorted, the gift of prophecy will be manifested. When there is sickness, there will be a need for the gifts of healing. When there are wrong spirits, there will be a need for the discerning of spirits. The gifts are in the church for the welfare of the church, and as needs arise, the Holy Spirit will manifest the appropriate gifts to meet the needs.

D. APPLICATION OF TRUTH

We may wholly trust the Holy Spirit to meet the needs in the life of a church or an individual by bearing the fruit or giving the needed gift. However, we must yield to the Spirit so that the Holy Spirit will have freedom to work and minister.

V. WE CAN CLASSIFY THE GIFTS OF THE SPIRIT IN THREE GROUPS

A. STATEMENT OF SCRIPTURE

"Now there are diversities of gifts, but the same Spirit.

And there are differences of administrations, but the same Lord. And there are diversities of operations, but it is the same God which worketh all in all" (I Corinthians 12:4-6).

B. STATEMENT OF TRUTH

In order to understand the gifts of the Spirit it is possible to classify the nine gifts under three headings.

C. EXPOSITION OF TRUTH

We may classify the gifts two different ways:

1. *According to the action involved*

a. Gifts of knowledge (to know): word of wisdom, word of knowledge, discerning of spirits.

b. Gifts of power (to act): faith, working of miracles, gifts of healing.

c. Gifts of utterance (to speak): prophecy, divers kinds of tongues, interpretation of tongues.

2. *According to I Corinthians 12:4-6*

a. Diversities of gifts: gifts of healing, prophecy, divers kinds of tongues, interpretation of tongues.

b. Differences of administrations: word of wisdom, word of knowledge, discerning of spirits.

c. Diversities of operations: faith, working of miracles.

D. APPLICATION OF TRUTH

By classifying the gifts we are able to understand them better and see the purpose of the Holy Spirit in manifesting them in the church.

VI. THERE ARE DEFINITE SINS AGAINST THE HOLY SPIRIT

A. STATEMENT OF SCRIPTURE

1. "Ye do always resist the Holy Ghost" (Acts 7:51).

2. "And hath done despite unto the Spirit of grace" (Hebrews 10:29).

3. "But the blasphemy against the Holy Ghost shall not be forgiven unto men" (Matthew 12:31).

4. "And grieve not the holy Spirit of God" (Ephesians 4:30).

5. "Quench not the Spirit" (I Thessalonians 5:19).

6. "Satan filled thine heart to lie to the Holy Ghost" (Acts 5:3).

B. STATEMENT OF TRUTH

There are definite sins against the Holy Spirit that may hinder the Holy Spirit from working in a person's life and that may cause him to lose his soul.

C. EXPOSITION OF TRUTH

Since the church is a Spirit-filled body and the work and ministry of the Holy Spirit in the church is so important, it is fitting to study sins that one can commit against the Holy Spirit. By sinning against the Holy Spirit a person may hinder the Spirit from working in the church, and he may even lose his own soul. Here is a list of sins against the Holy Spirit:

1. *Resisting the Holy Ghost* (Acts 7:51). This is the sin of rejection, and a sinner may commit it when the Holy Spirit deals with him. The sinner may reject until the Spirit no longer deals with him, for God's Spirit will not always strive with humanity (Genesis 6:3).

2. *Despising the Holy Spirit* (Hebrews 10:29). A study of the context makes clear that a backslider may commit this sin if he has contempt for what God has done for him. Esau's actions illustrate this sin. He despised his birthright and therefore found no place of repentance (Hebrews 12:17).

3. *Blaspheming the Holy Spirit* (Matthew 12:31-32). This is the unpardonable sin. It is committed by word, but Christ made clear that out of the abundance of the heart the mouth speaks (Matthew 12:34). It seems that the only

way to commit this sin is by speech prompted by a heart that despises the Holy Spirit. It consists of attributing to Satan the work and manifestation of the Holy Spirit, even though the person has every reason to know the reality of the Spirit's work. Here is a solemn warning to everyone to be careful how he judges the manifestation of the Holy Spirit.

4. *Grieving the Holy Spirit* (Ephesians 4:30). This sin concerns fruit bearing and the life of holiness. The Holy Spirit is easily grieved with careless, worldly living.

5. *Quenching the Holy Spirit* (I Thessalonians 5:19). This has to do with the operation of the gifts of the Spirit, with ministry and service. To quench means to put out a fire. This takes place when someone refuses to allow the Holy Spirit to have His way in ministry, in witnessing, in the gifts of the Spirit, and so on.

6. *Lying to the Holy Spirit* (Acts 5:3-4). This sin is related to consecration and surrender. It is professing a consecration that we know we do not possess. Ananias and Sapphira died, not because they kept back part of the price of their land, but because they falsely said they had brought it all, while keeping back part of it. Peter also said they tempted the Holy Spirit (Acts 5:9).

D. APPLICATION OF TRUTH

Salvation from beginning to end is entirely of the Spirit of God. From the time a person comes under conviction of sin to the moment he is resurrected or raptured (Romans 8:11), it is all by the Holy Spirit. How important it then becomes for a person to yield himself fully to the influence and power of the Holy Ghost. By sinning against God's Spirit in some way, a person may hinder the Holy Spirit from working and may easily lose his own soul. On the other hand, if he yields to the Spirit, he permits the Holy Spirit to perfect the will of God in his own life and that of the church.

QUESTIONS

1. Name the nine fruit of the Spirit.
2. Name the nine gifts of the Spirit.
3. Explain how the church is the "body of Christ."
4. Explain how salvation is the work of the Holy Spirit.
5. If the Holy Spirit bears one of the nine fruit, how many more will He bear?
6. What is New Testament prophecy?
7. What are the three different uses of speaking in tongues?
8. Explain the meaning of interpretation of tongues.
9. Name three ways in which the fruit of the Spirit and the gifts of the Spirit are similar.
10. Name five sins against the Holy Spirit.

PROJECTS

1. Write down each of the nine gifts of the Spirit, with a brief definition and explanation for each.
2. Do the necessary research and write a paper of not less than three hundred words on New Testament prophecy.

NOTES

Chapter 10

Christian Monotheism (Oneness)

I. THERE IS ONLY ONE GOD

A. STATEMENT OF SCRIPTURE

1. "Hear, O Israel: The LORD our God is one LORD" (Deuteronomy 6:4).

2. "Is there a God beside me? yea, there is no God; I know not any" (Isaiah 44:8).

3. "For there is one God, and one mediator between God and men, the man Christ Jesus" (I Timothy 2:5).

4. "Thou believest that there is one God; thou doest well: the devils also believe, and tremble" (James 2:19).

B. STATEMENT OF TRUTH

There is only one Supreme Being, who is God; He cannot be multiplied or pluralized.

C. EXPOSITION OF TRUTH

Possibly no other truth of Scripture receives more prominence than that of the oneness of God. Over fifty passages of Scripture teach that God is one and that there is no other. The very meaning of the term *God* signifies the supreme, almighty One. There can be but one ultimate, all-encompassing God. This is the great truth and message of the Old Testament, which the New Testament substantiates. The New Testament never contradicts this

Old Testament truth but rather fulfills it.

A multiplication of gods is a contradiction. God cannot be multiplied, and He is indivisible. If there could be even two gods, then there could be hundreds and thousands of gods. If there could be a second god, then Satan would not have fallen when he reached for equality with God. Likewise Adam and Eve would never have fallen when they exerted their own will in the act of disobedience. Although God is omniscient, there is one thing He does not know: He does not know another God (Isaiah 44:8).

The word *trinity* is not in the Bible. The doctrine of the trinity was introduced around A.D. 200 and was first officially endorsed in part by the Council of Nicea in A.D. 325. The Athanasian Creed later made the trinity a fundamental tenet. The doctrine of the trinity kept company with other Roman Catholic tenets such as transubstantiation, indulgences, Mariolatry, and so on. Unfortunately, when Protestants repudiated these fallacies they held on to the error of the trinity, maintaining a vital link with the false and unscriptural creeds of the Roman Catholic Church.

The word "persons," when used of the Godhead, does violence to the absolute oneness of God. Dividing God into three persons leads to belief in three gods, which is tritheism, regardless of how adherents may argue otherwise. The doctrine of the trinity leads to much confusion and contradiction.

D. APPLICATION OF TRUTH

Since our faith is built upon the foundation of our knowledge of God and His revelation of Himself to us, it is necessary to build upon the truth of the oneness of God. The trinity doctrine, which is a human tradition, will not stand in the day of judgment.

Since the trinity teaching came through the Roman

Catholic Church, we can expect that, as time passes, a line will be drawn more sharply between Oneness believers and those Protestants who will gradually merge back with the Roman Catholic Church.

E. DEFINITION OF TERMS

1. *Trinity*: A doctrine of the Roman Catholic Church that most Protestant groups have accepted. It states that there is one God divided into three persons who are coequal and coeternal. It is a contradiction and an impossibility.

2. *Transubstantiation*: A doctrine of the Roman Catholic Church that the bread and wine of the Lord's Supper are the literal body and blood of Christ.

3. *Indulgence*: An act of the Roman Catholic Church whereby it claims to cancel the temporal penalty for sin.

4. *Mariolatry*: The worship of Mary.

II. GOD IS SPIRIT

A. STATEMENT OF SCRIPTURE

1. "God is a Spirit: and they that worship him must worship him in spirit and in truth" (John 4:24).

2. "Behold, the heaven and heaven of heavens cannot contain thee" (I Kings 8:27).

3. "For a spirit hath not flesh and bones, as ye see me have" (Luke 24:39).

4. "Now unto the King eternal, immortal, invisible" (I Timothy 1:17).

B. STATEMENT OF TRUTH

God is Spirit and as such He has no physical limitations. We can see Him only in Jesus Christ.

C. EXPOSITION OF TRUTH

The Bible makes very clear that God is Spirit. Only

as Spirit can He be omnipresent, everywhere present at the same time, filling the universe. The Samaritan woman asked where people were to worship God—on Mt. Zion or Mt. Gerizim. Jesus answered that God is Spirit, and therefore people can worship Him everywhere. He is not to be confined to any one place. God is everywhere; the heaven and heaven of heavens cannot contain Him.

Since God is Spirit, He does not have any physical parts or bodily limitations. It is true that the Bible speaks of God as having hands, feet, arms, eyes, and ears; and it also says He sees, feels, and walks. Such expressions relative to God are human terms, which the Bible uses in order to bring the infinite within the comprehension of the finite. Only by means of human expressions can we understand God, the eternal Spirit.

However, God does have these physical parts in Christ Jesus. In Christ, God does have hands, feet, arms, and so on. Nevertheless, we must always remember that this is true only of God in Christ Jesus, God manifested in the flesh.

Since God is Spirit, He is invisible (Colossians 1:15; I Timothy 1:17). No one has seen God at any time (John 1:18). For this reason, God forbade the making of images for worship. No one has seen God, and nothing on earth can resemble Him. However, God manifested Himself in flesh (I Timothy 3:16). Jesus Christ is the express image of his person (Hebrews 1:3). As such, humans can see God in Jesus Christ. In fact, the only way that humans can see God is to see Him in Christ Jesus.

D. APPLICATION OF TRUTH

The most important fact here is that, since God is Spirit, we must worship Him in spirit and truth. Such worship is best offered by Spirit-filled people who have the revelation of the oneness of God and the almighty God in

Christ Jesus. We must also remember that we will see only *one* divine being in heaven.

E. DEFINITION OF TERMS

1. *Mt. Zion*: A mountain at Jerusalem.

2. *Mt. Gerizim*: A mountain in Samaria near Shechem, where the Samaritans built a temple.

III. GOD WAS MANIFEST IN THE FLESH

A. STATEMENT OF SCRIPTURE

1. "And without controversy great is the mystery of godliness: God was manifest in the flesh" (I Timothy 3:16).

2. "And the Word was made flesh and dwelt among us" (John 1:14).

3. "To wit, that God was in Christ, reconciling the world unto himself" (II Corinthians 5:19).

4. "For in him dwelleth all the fulness of the Godhead bodily" (Colossians 2:9).

B. STATEMENT OF TRUTH

In the Incarnation, the Word became flesh, and in that flesh the almighty God was manifest.

C. EXPOSITION OF TRUTH

1. *Incarnation.* The verb *incarnate* means to embody in flesh. In the Incarnation the Word became flesh (John 1:14), and God was manifest in the flesh (I Timothy 3:16). The Word was God, and in the Incarnation the Word became what He was not—flesh. Yet He became flesh without ceasing to be what He eternally was—God. As Spirit, God could not be born of Mary, but He did manifest Himself in flesh that was born of Mary. The flesh that was born was the Word incarnate. This does not make two persons, for the Word was God Himself.

We should note that in the Incarnation the Holy Ghost was the father of the baby who was born of the virgin Mary (Matthew 1:18-23). If the trinity theory were correct, and there were three persons in the Godhead, then the baby Jesus must have had two fathers. This, of course, is impossible. The one true God, who is Spirit, was the Father of the flesh that was born, and at the same time He manifested Himself in that flesh. One of the titles of Jesus Christ is Emmanuel, which means "God with us" (Matthew 1:23).

2. *Logos*. "Word" is a translation from the Greek *logos*, which means not only the expression of an inward thought but also the thought itself. We might say that the meaning of *Logos* in John 1 is "deity expressed." In other words, the *Logos* is the expression of the invisible God.

Just as we cannot separate a person's thinking and expression of that thinking from the person himself, and just as his thinking and expression are in essence his very being, not another person, so it is with God. John 1:1, written under inspiration to safeguard against the error of another person, clearly states that the *Logos* was God.

3. *God manifest in flesh.* One of the key verses of Scripture that we can only understand by divine illumination, and yet we must understand if we are to comprehend the doctrine of God, is I Timothy 3:16: "And without controversy great is the mystery of godliness: God was manifest in the flesh." The *Amplified Bible* reads: "He [God] was made visible in human flesh."

In the past God manifested Himself in many ways to humanity. In creation, on Mt. Sinai, in the theophanies (temporary visible manifestations of God), in the Tabernacle, and so on, people were able to receive a certain knowledge of God. However, in this verse of Scripture that speaks of God being manifested, we have the greatest knowledge of God ever given, for in the Incarnation Christ is the express image of the invisible God (Hebrews 1:3).

The mystery of godliness is God manifesting Himself

in flesh; the mystery of iniquity (II Thessalonians 2:7) is flesh manifesting itself as God. Scripture contrasts these two, and humans have a choice. If they do not accept the mystery of godliness, they will be compelled to accept the mystery of iniquity.

4. *The almighty God in Christ Jesus.* Scripture states that God was in Christ, reconciling the world to himself (II Corinthians 5:19). Once we understand this truth, the revelation of the oneness of the Godhead becomes clear. We see Jesus Christ as both God and man: God manifesting Himself in flesh, and God in that human temple reconciling the world to Himself. Are there two persons who are reconciling us to themselves? No, certainly not. "All things are of God, who hath reconciled us to himself by Jesus Christ" (II Corinthians 5:18).

5. *The fullness of the Godhead.* In Colossians 2:9 we read, "For in him dwelleth all the fulness of the Godhead bodily." Actually, we need no other verse of Scripture to prove the Oneness truth. Anyone who argues for the theory of the trinity must first clip this Scripture from his Bible. Let us examine this verse of Scripture by asking and answering a few questions:

a. Is Jesus in the Godhead or is the Godhead in Jesus? The trinitarians say that Jesus is in the Godhead; the Bible says that the Godhead is in Jesus.

b. Are there three fullnesses of the Godhead? Certainly not. There is only one fullness of the Godhead, who dwells in Jesus Christ.

c. Is only a part of the fullness of the Godhead in Jesus? The Bible says "all the fulness," not just a part of the fullness.

This verse of Scripture tells us that all the offices and attributes of God, the essence of His very being, are in Jesus Christ. It tells us that the only place we can find the Father is in Jesus Christ. Likewise, the only place we can find the Son and the Holy Ghost is in Jesus Christ.

D. APPLICATION OF TRUTH

The only way that a person can approach God and know the Father is through Christ Jesus. The only way that a person can see the Father is in Jesus Christ. When we see Him, we see the Father (John 14:9).

E. DEFINITION OF TERM

Theophanies: Manifestations of God in a visible form in the Old Testament.

IV. JESUS CHRIST IS BOTH GOD AND MAN

A. STATEMENT OF SCRIPTURE

1. "No man hath seen God at any time; the only begotten Son, which is in the bosom of the Father, he hath declared him" (John 1:18).

2. "And being found in fashion as a man, he humbled himself, and became obedient unto death, even the death of the cross" (Philippians 2:8).

3. "For there is one God, and one mediator between God and men, the man Christ Jesus" (I Timothy 2:5).

B. STATEMENT OF TRUTH

Jesus Christ possesses a dual nature: deity and humanity. He is the God-man: the true God and a perfect man united as one.

C. EXPOSITION OF TRUTH

In the Incarnation, Jesus Christ possessed a dual nature: deity and humanity. However, we should clearly understand that Jesus Christ was not two persons, nor did He possess two personalities. He was the God-man, the Word Incarnate, God manifest in flesh. As a human being, He was the Son; as God, He was the Father. As the Son, many times He spoke and acted as a man; as the Father, He spoke and acted as God.

Jesus Christ was the true God and a perfect man. We do not use the word *perfect* with deity, for there are no degrees of perfection with God, but there are degrees of perfection with humanity. Accordingly, it is proper to say that Jesus was the true God and a perfect man.

In His humanity, Jesus Christ was the Son of God. Sonship denotes a beginning and a relation to time and place. Only as He became a man was He able to become the only begotten Son (John 3:16). He was not an eternal son or a created son, but a Son that was conceived in the womb of Mary. As the Son, He grew, matured, and was subject to the Father. As the Son, He tasted of our infirmities and weaknesses and was tempted in every point.

The theory of the eternal Son is not scriptural. It came as the result of the trinitarian theory, and it teaches a second person in the Godhead. Jesus Christ in the flesh was the begotten Son. The words *begotten* and *eternal* mean the very opposite and contradict each other.

Jesus came in flesh as the Son for the following reasons:

1. That He might become our Redeemer. The Atonement demanded the offering of a sinless sacrifice in our stead. Only God could provide such a sacrifice (Hebrews 2:14).

2. That He might become our Mediator. Our Mediator knows our weaknesses through His omniscience and also actual human experience (Hebrews 4:15).

3. That He might become our King. In order to have a kingdom there must be a king. He reigns now in our hearts, but soon He shall come to reign upon this earth (Matthew 26:64).

4. That He might be our judge (Acts 17:31).

D. APPLICATION OF TRUTH

This glorious truth solves all problems concerning the

life and ministry of our Lord. It explains how He could be tempted, how He could pray, how He could die on Calvary, and so on. If anyone has difficulty in understanding just how Jesus Christ could occupy two offices at the same time, we can draw their attention to Isaiah 53:6: "The Lord hath laid on him the iniquity of us all." Who is the high priest? Who is the sacrificial Lamb who carries our iniquity? If Jesus Christ can be both priest and sacrifice at the same time, He also can be Father and Son, deity and humanity.

V. JESUS CHRIST POSSESSES THE ATTRIBUTES AND PREROGATIVES OF DEITY

A. STATEMENT OF SCRIPTURE

1. "All power is given unto me in heaven and in earth" (Matthew 28:18).
2. "In whom are hid all the treasures of wisdom and knowledge" (Colossians 2:3).
3. "For where two or three are gathered together in my name, there am I in the midst of them" (Matthew 18:20).
4. "Then came she and worshipped him" (Matthew 15:25).
5. "And he said unto her, Thy sins are forgiven" (Luke 7:48).
6. "All things were made by him" (John 1:3).

B. STATEMENT OF TRUTH

The Bible clearly reveals that Jesus Christ possesses both the attributes and the prerogatives of Deity. This fact conclusively proves the deity of Jesus Christ.

C. EXPOSITION OF TRUTH

We shall explain this truth by dealing with three attributes and three prerogatives. These should be sufficient to prove this proposition.

1. *Attributes*

a. *Omnipotence.* Jesus said that "all power" was given unto Him. He is "the Almighty" (Revelation 1:8) Can there possibly be two who are called "Almighty"? If Jesus has "all power," can there possibly be another who has "all power"? Jesus revealed His omnipotence over disease, death, nature, and demons.

b. *Omniscience.* Jesus knew what was in the human heart (John 2:24-25), and He knew all things (John 16:30). In Him are hid all the treasures of wisdom and knowledge. If He has all the treasures of wisdom and knowledge, certainly He must possess the attribute of omniscience.

c. *Omnipresence.* The only way He can be where His disciples are gathered together is to possess this attribute. Jesus Christ is everywhere at the same time.

2. *Prerogatives*

a. *The right to receive worship.* There was not the slightest reluctance on Christ's part to accept worship; therefore Jesus Christ is God, or He was an impostor. It was He who said, "Worship God only," and He had no right to take the place of God if He were not God. Nevertheless, even the angels are commanded to worship Him (Philippians 2:10; Hebrews 1:6).

b. *The right to forgive sins.* All sin is against God, and therefore, only God can forgive sin. For this reason the Pharisees charged Jesus with blasphemy. If Jesus Christ can forgive sin, then He must be God. On various occasions He did forgive sin (Mark 2:5; Luke 7:48).

c. *The right and power to create.* Jesus showed that He is the Creator by (1) turning water into wine (John 2:1-11); (2) feeding the five thousand (John 6:1-13); (3) walking on the water (John 6:19); and (4) quieting the storm (Mark 4:39). All things were made by Him (John 1:3). Are there two Creators? There can be only one, who is Jesus Christ.

D. APPLICATION OF TRUTH

That Jesus possesses the attributes and prerogatives of deity conclusively proves His deity, in spite of all the arguments of skeptics and unbelievers to the contrary.

E. DEFINITION OF TERMS

1. *Attribute*: A characteristic or quality.

2. *Prerogative:* An exclusive right or privilege attached to an office.

VI. JESUS IS THE NAME OF THE FATHER, SON, AND HOLY GHOST

A. STATEMENT OF SCRIPTURE

1. "In that day shall there be one LORD, and his name one" (Zechariah 14:9).

2. "And thou shalt call his name JESUS: for he shall save his people from their sins" (Matthew 1:21).

3. "Baptizing them in the name of the Father, and of the Son, and of the Holy Ghost" (Matthew 28:19).

4. "Neither is there salvation in any other: for there is none other name under heaven given among men, whereby we must be saved" (Acts 4:12).

B. STATEMENT OF TRUTH

The New Testament reveals God's saving name, which is Jesus. The name of the Father, Son, and Holy Ghost is Jesus.

C. EXPOSITION OF TRUTH

The prophet stated that there is one Lord and His name one (Zechariah 14:9). If we believe that there are three persons in the Godhead (three Gods), then we shall have to have three names. A person is identified by his name. However, the prophet stated that his name is one. In the great commission, as recorded in Matthew 28:19, the name is singular. What is that name? We find the answer in Acts 4:12. There is no other name.

There are many titles of our God, which depict His offices and characteristics. Among them are the titles of Father, Son, and Holy Ghost. In like manner, a person is body, soul, and spirit, but these are not the person's name. Would a bank cash a check that carries the signature "Body, soul, and spirit"? We know that the check must carry his signature, which is his name. At one time the author was his son's schoolteacher and his pastor. To his son he was father, pastor, and teacher. These were three titles, but none of them was his name. Even so, Father, Son, and Holy Ghost are not names but titles.

The testimony of Scripture is overwhelming, stating clearly the truth and leaving no room for even a shadow of doubt that the name of deity is Jesus. We will make no attempt here to give a comprehensive study of this marvelous truth, but the following passages of Scripture will convince the honest heart:

a. "I am come in my Father's name" (John 5:43).

b. "I have declared unto them thy name" (John 17:26).

c. "Who art thou, Lord [Jehovah]? And the Lord [Jehovah] said, I am Jesus" (Acts 9:5).

d. "Stephen, calling upon God . . . saying Lord Jesus" (Acts 7:59).

e. "A name which is above every name" (Philippians 2:9).

D. APPLICATION OF TRUTH

There is no other name under heaven whereby we must be saved (Acts 4:12). Jesus is the saving name of our God. It is quite evident that we obey Matthew 28:19 only when we baptize a person into the name of Jesus. In fact, whatever we do in word or deed we must do in the name of Jesus (Colossians 3:17).

QUESTIONS

1. State three attributes of deity that Jesus Christ possesses.
2. Explain how the doctrine of the trinity leads to tritheism.
3. In teaching primary children, what basic truth concerning deity would you teach first?
4. Explain the meaning of the Incarnation.
5. Why must we worship God in spirit and truth?
6. Explain the meaning of *logos*.
7. What is the purpose of the Son?
8. Explain how Jesus was able to pray.
9. How did Jesus show that He is the Creator?
10. What is the name of the Father, Son, and Holy Ghost?

PROJECTS

1. Do the necessary research and then outline the method by which you would deal with an atheist.
2. Make a list of twenty titles of Jesus, giving chapter and verse where each is found.

NOTES

Chapter 11

The Second Coming of Christ

I. GOD'S WORD CLEARLY PROMISES THE SECOND COMING OF JESUS

A. STATEMENT OF SCRIPTURE

1. "For I know that my redeemer liveth, and that he shall stand at the latter day upon the earth" (Job 19:25).

2. "I will come again, and receive you unto myself; that where I am, there ye may be also" (John 14:3).

3. "This same Jesus, which is taken up from you into heaven, shall so come in like manner as ye have seen him go into heaven" (Acts 1:11).

4. "For the Lord himself shall descend from heaven with a shout" (I Thessalonians 4:16).

B. STATEMENT OF TRUTH

The Scriptures repeat the promise of the Lord's return to earth over and over again, until there can be no possible mistake concerning this glorious promise.

C. EXPOSITION OF TRUTH

The doctrine of the second coming of Christ is one of the most important doctrines of the Bible. The greater number of predictions concerning Christ in the Old Testament refer to His second coming. Some have estimated that the Bible mentions the Second Coming six to eight times as often as Christ's first coming. Paul referred to it at least fifty times in his epistles. According to one count, the New Testament mentions in 318 times in its 260 chapters. The Bible devotes whole chapters to this doctrine.

It is not practical to list the many verses of Scripture that promise Christ's second coming. We will mention just a few of them here to show the clear testimony of prophecy in this regard from Genesis to Revelation.

1. *Jacob's prophecy* (Genesis 49:10). Jacob's prophecy mentions both advents of Christ. It refers to the Second Advent by speaking of the "gathering of the people" to Him.

2. *Job's prophecy* (Job 19:25). Job associated the appearance of Christ upon earth with the resurrection.

3. *Zechariah's prophecy* (Zechariah 14:4). Here we find that Jesus shall return to the Mount of Olives.

4. *The promise of Jesus* (John 14:3; Revelation 22:7, 12, 20). Jesus made a definite promise of returning and receiving His children to Himself.

5. *The promise of two angels* (Acts 1:11). What do we need more than the promise of two messengers from heaven?

6. *Paul's prophecy* (I Thessalonians 4:16). This is only one of many verses of Scripture where the apostle Paul describes the Second Coming.

7. *Peter's prophecy* (II Peter 3:3-14). The apostle Peter warned against scoffers and exhorted that we should be ready for the Lord's coming.

8. *John's prophecy* (I John 3:2-3). The apostle John clearly expresses the hope of the church.

9. *The prophecy of Revelation* (Revelation 3:11). The entire Book of Revelation deals with the events connected with the return of the Lord.

D. APPLICATION OF TRUTH

When Scripture gives such a prominent place to a truth,

we should give special attention to it. There should be no doubt in our minds regarding the second coming of Christ, and we should make all preparation for that great event.

II. THE SECOND COMING OF CHRIST IS LITERAL

A. STATEMENT OF SCRIPTURE

1. "This same Jesus, which is taken up from you into heaven, shall so come in like manner as ye have seen him go into heaven" (Acts 1:11).

2. "For the Lord himself shall descend from heaven with a shout" (I Thessalonians 4:16).

3. "Behold, he cometh with clouds; and every eye shall see him, and they also which pierced him" (Revelation 1:7).

B. STATEMENT OF TRUTH

The second coming of Jesus is a personal, visible, and literal return. It does not mean death, the coming of the Holy Spirit at Pentecost, the destruction of Jerusalem, or anything other than a literal return of Christ.

C. EXPOSITION OF TRUTH

The following passages of Scripture reveal that the second coming of Jesus is personal, visible, and literal:

1. "I will come again" (John 14:3).

2. "This same Jesus . . . shall so come in like manner as ye have seen him go into heaven" (Acts 1:11).

3. "For the Lord himself shall descend" (I Thessalonians 4:16).

4. "Every eye shall see him" (Revelation 1:7).

5. "Behold, I come quickly" (Revelation 22:7).

People have made many attempts to spiritualize the return of Jesus, but we can easily show that all such attempts have no scriptural foundation. Here we examine a few such attempts.

1. *The Second Coming does not mean death.*

a. Christ's first coming did not mean death to the Jews; neither does His second coming mean death to the saints.

b. Death is an enemy, but at Christ's coming we will rise from the dead and shout victory over death (I Corinthians 15:55).

c. The Christian does not look forward to death, but the coming of Jesus is the church's hope. We do not long to be unclothed but rather to be clothed (II Corinthians 5:4).

d. The following verses of Scripture have no meaning if we substitute "death" for the Second Coming: John 21:22; Matthew 16:28; Philippians 3:20.

2. *The Second Coming does not mean the coming of the Holy Spirit.*

a. Many promises of the Second Coming were after the coming of the Holy Spirit at Pentecost (Philippians 3:21; II Timothy 4:8; I Thessalonians 4:16; I Corinthians 15:51).

b. At Pentecost, Christ did not receive us to Himself but came to us spiritually.

c. The events of I Thessalonians 4:16-17 did not occur on the Day of Pentecost or when we received the Holy Ghost.

3. *The Second Coming does not refer to the destruction of Jerusalem.*

a. The events of I Thessalonians 4:16-17 did not take place at that time.

b. John 21:21-23 and Revelation 22:20 were written after the destruction of Jerusalem.

D. APPLICATION OF TRUTH

Since the second coming of Christ is literal, visible, and personal, we should accept as literal all the other events associated with His return such as the rapture of the church. Let us never be guilty of spiritualizing passages of Scripture that we should accept literally.

E. DEFINITION OF TERMS

1. *Literal*: Following the exact meaning of the words.

2. *Spiritualize*: To make "spiritual" by interpreting words to mean something besides what they state literally.

3. *Rapture of the church*: The catching away of the living saints without their experiencing death.

III. THE SECOND COMING OF CHRIST IS PREMILLENNIAL

A. STATEMENT OF SCRIPTURE

1. "Let both grow together until the harvest . . . gather the wheat into my barn" (Matthew 13:30).

2. "Immediately after the tribulation of those days . . . then shall appear the sign of the Son of man" (Matthew 24:29-30).

3. "And then shall that Wicked be revealed, whom the Lord shall consume with the spirit of his mouth, and shall destroy with the brightness of his coming" (II Thessalonians 2:8).

B. STATEMENT OF TRUTH

The second coming of Jesus will precede the Millennium.

C. EXPOSITION OF TRUTH

The Bible clearly teaches premillennialism, in sharp contrast to two errors that have crept into the church world: postmillennialism and amillennialism. The first of these two errors, postmillennialism, teaches that the church will prosper and grow until the world shall be converted, bringing in the Millennium, and then afterwards Jesus shall return to earth. The other error teaches that there will be no Millennium and that the second advent of Christ will destroy this world. Both of these errors leave no room for the second coming of Jesus to be the blessed hope of the church. The Scriptures are very plain in their teaching that the second advent of our Lord will occur before the Millennium and that the return of our Lord is the blessed and living hope of the church.

We should keep clearly in mind that the Bible reveals two phases in the second coming of our Lord. Just as there were two phases in His first advent (first, in bodily form to all, then in His resurrection body to His chosen disciples), there will be two phases in His second advent. They will be in reverse order to that of His first advent. In His return He will first come *for* His saints, and then later He will come *with* His saints. Both of these comings are premillennial.

The first phase is the appearance of Jesus in the air only to catch His church out of this world. He comes for His saints to return into glory with them. The same Greek word translated "to meet" is used in I Thessalonians 4:17 and Acts 28:15. It means a going forth in order to return with. This thought is clearly brought out in the first phase of our Lord's return. It is known as the rapture of the church, and it is the blessed hope of the saints.

The second phase is the appearance of Jesus to execute judgment when He returns to reign and to set up His millennial kingdom. The passages of Scripture used in this section to prove premillennialism have reference to this second phase of the coming of the Lord. Let us remember that the first phase of the Lord's advent, when He comes for His saints, must precede the second phase, when He returns with His saints to reign. Therefore, if we can prove the Lord's return in judgment to be premillennial, then definitely His return for the church is also premillennial.

Here are a few reasons why premillennialism is right:

1. The Millennium is a literal reign of Jesus (Isaiah 32:1; Jeremiah 3:17; Zechariah 14:16). Therefore Jesus must come before the Millennium.

2. The true church will be a persecuted, suffering, cross-bearing people until Jesus comes (John 15:19-21;

I Thessalonians 3:3; II Timothy 3:12). Nowhere does the Scripture teach that the world is going to be converted by the efforts of the church.

3. The Antichrist, who is premillennial, will be destroyed by the brightness of Christ's coming (II Thessalonians 2:8).

4. The Tribulation is premillennial, and Jesus will come to set up His kingdom "immediately after" that time (Matthew 24:29-31). This passage refers to the second phase of the Lord's return, when He returns with His saints to reign. This is conclusive proof that the Lord's coming in the air to catch away His bride is also premillennial. The Scriptures indicate that Jesus will come for His church at the beginning of the Tribulation and return with His church to reign at the end of the Tribulation.

5. Tares and wheat grow together until the end of the age (Matthew 13:24-30). This world will never be entirely converted in this church age.

D. APPLICATION OF TRUTH

We should not look for the world to become better and better, but rather we should look up for the return of our Lord (Luke 21:28). The world will get worse and worse until this age ends by our Lord's return.

E. DEFINITION OF TERM

Millennium: The literal, glorious reign of Christ upon earth for one thousand years.

IV. THE SECOND COMING OF CHRIST IS THE HOPE OF THE CHURCH

A. STATEMENT OF SCRIPTURE

1. "Looking for that blessed hope, and glorious appearing of the great God and our Saviour Jesus Christ" (Titus 2:13).

2. "God . . . hath begotten us again unto a lively hope" (I Peter 1:3).

3. "And every man that hath this hope in him purifieth himself, even as he is pure" (I John 3:3).

B. STATEMENT OF TRUTH

The church has no greater hope than the coming of Jesus. This hope sanctifies and comforts the church and gives her a real anchor in this troubled world.

C. EXPOSITION OF TRUTH

Possibly no other message affects the church as much as the message of Christ's return. This truth gives the church a real hope that comforts and sanctifies her and gives her a solid anchor during times of trouble. No child of God longs for death because death is an enemy, but the child of God does look forward to and long for the coming of Jesus with joyful anticipation. At this time there will be a resurrection of the saints who have previously died, and the living saints will be translated to meet their Lord in the clouds of glory. We may describe this hope of the church as follows:

1. It is a blessed hope (Titus 2:13).
2. It is a comforting hope (I Thessalonians 4:18).
3. It is a living hope (I Peter 1:3).
4. It is a purifying hope (I John 3:3).
5. It is an anchor of the soul (Hebrews 6:19).
6. It does not disappoint (Romans 5:5).

The apostle Paul explained the longing of the church to see Jesus, at which time she will be clothed with immortality. This longing is not for death but for the second coming of Christ (II Corinthians 5:1-4).

D. APPLICATION OF TRUTH

When we realize the nearness of the coming of Jesus, our hearts are thrilled with anticipation and expectation with the thought of seeing the Lord. Not only does the thought fill our hearts with gladness, it keeps us praying, witnessing, and living dedicated, holy lives—ready at any moment to rise to meet Him in the clouds.

V. JESUS WILL RETURN FOR THOSE WHO ARE READY

A. STATEMENT OF SCRIPTURE

1. "Therefore be ye also ready" (Matthew 24:44).

2. "That he might present it to himself a glorious church, not having spot, or wrinkle, or any such thing; but that it should be holy and without blemish" (Ephesians 5:27).

3. "Follow peace with all men, and holiness, without which no man shall see the Lord" (Hebrews 12:14).

B. STATEMENT OF TRUTH

Jesus will return for a church that is ready for His coming; a definite preparation is necessary to be ready for His return.

C. EXPOSITION OF TRUTH

Since Jesus ascended into heaven He has been preparing a place for His bride. Here on earth He also has been preparing a beautiful bride to enter that prepared place. We must realize that New Jerusalem is a prepared place for a prepared people. No sin will enter there. Jesus will not catch away a people who are in the process of getting ready. He will return for a people who are ready, who have fully obeyed the New Testament message of salvation and are living godly lives.

It is useless to enter into arguments concerning who will be raptured and who will not. Rather, we should allow the Scriptures speak for themselves. For this reason, we list here the passages of Scripture that refer to this extremely important matter:

1. A *glorious church without spot or wrinkle*. "That he might present it to himself a glorious church, not having spot, or wrinkle, or any such thing" (Ephesians 5:27).

2. *Those who are "in Christ."* "The dead in Christ shall rise first" (I Thessalonians 4:16). We must be "in Christ" to be ready for the Rapture.

3. *Baptized into His body*. "For by one Spirit are we all baptized into one body" (I Corinthians 12:13). The Holy Ghost places us into the body, which is His church.

4. *The Holy Spirit will quicken our bodies*. "He that raised up Christ from the dead shall also quicken your mortal bodies by his Spirit that dwelleth in you" (Romans 8:11). It is the Holy Ghost who will quicken our bodies at the Rapture.

5. *Oil in our lamps*. The parable of the ten virgins (Matthew 25:1-13) teaches the necessity of being ready for the coming of the Bridegroom, indicating that we must be full of the Holy Ghost.

6. *The name of Jesus is necessary*. "To take out of them a people for his name" (Acts 15:14). Jesus is taking a Gentile bride to bear His name.

7. *Holiness is essential*. "Follow peace with all men, and holiness, without which no man shall see the Lord" (Hebrews 12:14). Only those who are holy may have this blessed hope.

8. *We must be looking for His return*. "Unto them that look for him shall he appear the second time without sin unto salvation" (Hebrews 9:28). Only those who are ready will actually be looking for His return.

9. *We must walk with the Lord*. "And Enoch walked with God: and he was not; for God took him" (Genesis 5:24). Enoch, a type of the church, walked with God and was raptured.

D. APPLICATION OF TRUTH

Jesus exhorted us always to be ready, for we do not

know the hour He will return. The scripturally correct attitude for the New Testament saint is: (a) Jesus may come *now*; and (b) I am ready to go *now*. He walks in all the light he knows, obeys fully, and is always ready.

VI. THE SECOND COMING OF JESUS IS IMMINENT

A. STATEMENT OF SCRIPTURE

1. "Therefore be ye also ready: for in such an hour as ye think not the Son of man cometh" (Matthew 24:44).

2. "And when these things begin to come to pass, then look up, and lift up your heads; for your redemption draweth nigh" (Luke 21:28).

3. "And that, knowing the time, that now it is high time to awake out of sleep: for now is our salvation nearer than when we believed" (Romans 13:11).

B. STATEMENT OF TRUTH

No one knows the exact time, but every sign indicates that the coming of Jesus is imminent.

C. EXPOSITION OF TRUTH

It is evident that the sun is setting upon this age and that the Lord is about to return for His waiting bride. Not only students of prophecy, but also students of world events, know that momentous days are ahead, that this world is in a period of transition, and that the present religious, social, and political orders will not continue. In the mind of the unbeliever, there can only be a question mark and an uneasy foreboding; but in the heart of the child of God there is a joyful anticipation. One of the most startling and impressive facts is that more prophecy has been fulfilled in our generation than in all the centuries since Christ's first advent. Surely this should convince everyone that it cannot be long, that time's clock is striking the hour. The following abbreviated list contains a few of the signs of the times:

1. *God's week in dealing with humanity* (II Peter 3:8). We are drawing to the close of the sixth day in God's week; the seventh will be Christ's literal reign upon earth.

2. *The latter-rain outpouring* (James 5:7). Since the beginning of the twentieth century the Lord has baptized millions with the Holy Ghost, restored apostolic truth to many, and brought many back to the apostolic doctrine and experience.

3. *The Laodicean church and apostasy* (Revelation 3:16; Matthew 24:24; II Thessalonians 2:3; I Timothy 4:1; II Timothy 3:1-5; 4:3-4; II Peter 2:1-2; Jude 4).

4. *Increase of crime, immorality, and juvenile delinquency* (Luke 17:26-30; II Timothy 3:1-7). Crime has been increasing four to five times faster than the population. Our land is flooded with filth and pornography, and juvenile delinquency is appalling.

5. *Increase of restlessness and increase of travel* (Daniel 12:4).

6. *Increase of knowledge* (Daniel 12:4). Human knowledge is increasing at the same rate as the population explosion. Within the last few years the amount of human knowledge has doubled.

7. *The atomic and space age* (Revelation 6:12-17). In 1905 Albert Einstein wrote a mathematical equation, $e = mc^2$, that has changed the entire world. Humans can now generate as much energy from one cubic inch of uranium as from 250,000 gallons of fuel oil.

8. *Political and social troubles* (Luke 21:25-26; James 5:1-6).

9. *Confederation of the northern nations* (Ezekiel 38 and 39). This prophecy apparently pictures Russia and confederate nations.

10. *Consolidation of western powers.* The European Community and Western alliances seem to fulfill certain

portions of Daniel's prophecy.

11. *One world church.* The ecumenical movements, both with the Roman Catholic Church and the World Council of Churches, are preparing the way for one world church in fulfillment of prophecies in Revelation 17.

12. *Israel* (Luke 21:29-31; Romans 11:25). The Jew is said to be God's clock. That the nation of Israel was formed in 1948 is sufficient proof of the end times.

D. APPLICATION OF TRUTH

The application of this truth to our lives is very plain. There can be no delay in our preparation for His return; being ready to meet the Lord is urgent business in every individual's life. Knowing just how imminent the Lord's return really is, "what manner of persons ought ye to be in all holy conversation and godliness?" (II Peter 3:11).

E. DEFINITION OF TERMS

1. *Pornography*: Obscene and filthy literature and pictures.

2. *Ecumenical movement*: The movement to unite all the professing churches throughout the world.

QUESTIONS

1. Why is the doctrine of the second coming of Christ important?
2. Show that the return of Jesus will be literal.
3. What is the Millennium?
4. Explain the term *premillennialism.*
5. What is the hope of the church?
6. For whom is Jesus returning?
7. How do we know that the second coming of Jesus is imminent?
8. What is the ecumenical movement?
9. Show that there are two phases in the Second Advent.

10. When may the rapture of the church take place?

PROJECTS

1. Write a paper of at least three hundred words on the the necessary preparation of the church for the coming of Jesus.

2. Cut out at least ten clippings from recent newspapers and magazines to show fulfilled prophecy relating to the end times.

NOTES

Chapter 12
The Last Things

I. THERE IS COMING THE GREAT TRIBULATION, WHICH WILL END AT THE BATTLE OF ARMAGEDDON

A. STATEMENT OF SCRIPTURE

1. "For then shall be great tribulation, such as was not since the beginning of the world to this time, no, nor ever shall be" (Matthew 24:21).

2. "And there shall be a time of trouble, such as never was since there was a nation even to that same time" (Daniel 12:1).

3. "To gather them to the battle of that great day of God Almighty. . . . And he gathered them together into a place called in the Hebrew tongue Armageddon" (Revelation 16:14-16).

B. STATEMENT OF TRUTH

This age will close with a period of unprecedented trouble, which will terminate at the Battle of Armageddon.

C. EXPOSITION OF TRUTH

In the past there have been many periods of intense persecution and tribulation for both the Jews and the church. However, our Lord spoke of a time at the close of this age that is known as the Tribulation. So that we would not mistake this period of tribulation for any that has already taken place in history, Jesus said that He would return to set up His kingdom *immediately* after it (Matthew 24:29). He also stated that this tribulation would be greater than anything that preceded it.

As we carefully study prophecy the Word of God, we come to the conclusion that the Tribulation is a period of time when the world is plunged into spiritual darkness, great upheaval, severe chastisement, and terrible judgment. As the time of the Tribulation advances, God's judgments upon earth are intensified. The last three and one-half years (Revelation 11:2-3; 12:14; 13:5-6) are when the rule of the Antichrist ("the beast") culminates.

This terrible time of trouble and judgment will terminate at the Battle of Armageddon (Revelation 16:14-16). At this time Jesus Christ will come back in judgment to set up His kingdom upon earth (Matthew 25:31; II Thessalonians 1:7-10).

D. APPLICATION OF TRUTH

As we look forward to the days of great trouble just ahead, when the judgments of God will come upon the earth, we realize how important it is to be ready for Christ's return and to warn everyone of the impending storms. If our lives are hid with Christ in God (Colossians 3:3), we have nothing to fear. The true, safe hiding place is in the name of the Lord (Proverbs 18:10).

E. DEFINITION OF TERM

Armageddon: The ancient hill and valley of Megiddo, west of the Jordan in the plain of Jezreel.

II. IN THE MILLENNIUM, JESUS SHALL REIGN FOR ONE THOUSAND YEARS

A. STATEMENT OF SCRIPTURE

1. "He . . . bound him a thousand years. . . . They lived

and reigned with Christ a thousand years . . . and shall reign with him a thousand years" (Revelation 20:1-7).

2. "He shall rule them with a rod of iron" (Revelation 19:15).

3. "And the LORD shall be king over all the earth: in that day shall there be one LORD, and his name one" (Zechariah 14:9).

B. STATEMENT OF TRUTH

There will be a literal reign of Christ upon earth for one thousand years.

C. EXPOSITION OF TRUTH

The Millennium means the thousand-year reign of Christ upon earth. God is dealing with the human family in several ages, of which the Millennium is the last. It will be the seventh day in God's week in His dealings with humanity; the Millennium will be the Sabbath (day of rest) for this troubled world. In this present church age our Sabbath is the Holy Ghost (the presence of Jesus Christ Himself) abiding and reigning in our hearts. True rest only comes as Jesus Christ reigns supreme. In the Millennium it will be a literal reign, and a literal peace and rest that the nations remaining upon the earth will enjoy.

The Millennium begins at the coming of Christ with His saints, with the revelation of Christ after the Tribulation. At this time Christ will bring judgment to Antichrist and the enemies of God's people. He will bind Satan and cast him into the bottomless pit.

During the Millennium Christ will "reign with a rod of iron," implying that His divine power will hold in restraint the effects of the curse. Much of the curse upon nature will be removed, but not all of its effects will be brought to an end until the new heaven and new earth following the Millennium. The Millennium will be a time of blessedness such as this world has never seen. There will be universal peace among the nations, and there will be no satanic temptation.

The Millennium will terminate at the end of the thousand-year period, with Satan being set free. Immediately there will be a fresh rebellion against God, proving that Satan has not changed and that human nature cannot stand alone. This rebellion will quickly come to an end, and Christ will bring in a new and eternal order, never to be invaded by sin, the flesh, the world, or the devil. In the new earth, "there shall be no more curse" (Revelation 22:3). At this time the statement of the apostle Paul in I Corinthians 15:24-28 will be completely fulfilled.

D. APPLICATION OF TRUTH

Soon every knee shall bow at the name of Jesus, and every tongue shall confess that Jesus Christ is Lord (Philippians 2:10-11). How much better to do it voluntarily now! The kingdom of God will be set up and Jesus will reign supreme some day. We have the choice of meeting judgment at that day or reigning with Him. If we crown Him King of our lives now, and allow Him to set up the kingdom of God in our hearts now, we shall have the joy of entering with Him into His glorious reign.

III. THE FINAL JUDGMENT WILL BE AT THE GREAT WHITE THRONE

A. STATEMENT OF SCRIPTURE

1. "Who shall judge the quick and the dead at his appearing and his kingdom" (II Timothy 4:1).

2. "And as it is appointed unto men once to die, but after this the judgment" (Hebrews 9:27).

3. "And I saw a great white throne. . . . And whosoever was not found written in the book of life was cast into the lake of fire" (Revelation 20:11-15).

B. STATEMENT OF TRUTH

The Great White Throne will be the scene of the final judgment when people will be judged on whether or not their names are in the Book of Life.

C. EXPOSITION OF TRUTH

All sin must be judged; no one will escape judgment. Through repentance, obedience, and faith it is possible to have our sins judged at Calvary. If sin is not remitted here in this life, it will follow the individual into eternity. God's first judgment for sin is at Calvary; God's final judgment for sin is at the Great White Throne.

At this time there will take place a resurrection of all people who did not have part in the first resurrection. All who are raised in this resurrection stand before God, and the books are opened. It appears that these books consist of:

1. The Word of God (the Bible).
2. God's books of remembrance (which describe the works of people).
3. The Lamb's Book of Life (Revelation 21:27).

This judgment will determine the eternal destiny of each person, solely on the basis of whether or not his name is in the Book of Life. The supreme question will be: "Are you in the Book of Life?"

D. APPLICATION OF TRUTH

Possibly the main thing to remember here is that no one shall escape judgment. Just as death is certain, judgment is certain. Sooner or later it will come to everyone. How important it is to have our sins remitted now!

IV. THE ETERNAL DESTINY OF THE WICKED IS THE LAKE OF FIRE

A. STATEMENT OF SCRIPTURE

1. "Depart from me, ye cursed, into everlasting fire,

prepared for the devil and his angels" (Matthew 25:41).

2. "For the wages of sin is death" (Romans 6:23).

3. "This is the second death. And whosoever was not found written in the book of life was cast into the lake of fire" (Revelation 20:14-15).

B. STATEMENT OF TRUTH

The wicked will be throughout eternity in the lake of fire, which was prepared for the devil and his angels.

C. EXPOSITION OF TRUTH

The destiny of the wicked is eternal separation from God and the eternal suffering of His wrath. This is known as the second death. Because of its terrible nature, it is a subject from which we naturally shrink; yet it is one which we must face, because it is positive truth of divine revelation. The Christ of gentleness and love warned people against the sufferings of hell.

The "second death" does not mean cessation of existence any more than the "new birth" means the beginning of existence. Eternal life does not mean to live forever, but to live in a state of blessedness forever. Eternal life does not deal with quantity as much as with quality of existence. Just so with eternal death. It is a quality of existence, not cessation of being. Even in this life, death can coexist with life (Ephesians 2:1). What people call life God calls death. There are two things the child of God receives: at the new birth, eternal life; at the resurrection, immortality, even though he already had existence. So it is in the case of the wicked. The second death does not mean cessation of existence, for he is dead now in this life. It means eternal separation from God.

Hell was never prepared for humans. God made it for the devil and his followers. God has done everything He can do to stop people from going to this dreadful place, short of violating their will. The cross of Calvary is a roadblock, stopping humans from their slide into a lost eternity. Christ died to stop men and women from going there. If a person willfully chooses to be a follower of Satan, he definitely will be with Satan throughout eternity.

The Scriptures describe the nature of hell as follows:

1. Extreme suffering (Revelation 20:10).
2. Memory still active (Luke 16:25).
3. Unsatisfied desire (Luke 16:24).
4. Remorse (Luke 16:27-28).
5. Shame with contempt (Daniel 12:2).
6. The worm does not die (Mark 9:46).
7. The fire is not quenched (Mark 9:46).
8. Bottomless (Revelation 20:3).
9. Darkness (Matthew 25:30).
10. No rest (Revelation 14:11).

There will be no light, no music, no honor, no hope in hell. What a dreadful, fearful place!

D. APPLICATION OF TRUTH

When we consider the awful darkness and fearfulness of a lost eternity, how thankful every redeemed soul should be for salvation! How urgent salvation becomes for every unsaved man and woman! How significant the gospel becomes, and how important the great commission becomes to the church! What a heavy responsibility every child of God has to point men and women to Jesus Christ!

V. THE ETERNAL HOME OF THE CHURCH WILL BE NEW JERUSALEM

A. STATEMENT OF SCRIPTURE

1. "In my Father's house are many mansions: if it were not so, I would have told you. I go to prepare a place for you" (John 14:2).

2. "And I John saw the holy city, new Jerusalem, coming down from God out of heaven, prepared as a bride

adorned for her husband" (Revelation 21:2).

B. STATEMENT OF TRUTH

Jesus Christ has prepared the holy city, New Jerusalem, to be the eternal home of the church. The saints shall dwell eternally in the presence of Jesus Christ.

C. EXPOSITION OF TRUTH

This world is not the home of the church. She is only a pilgrim and a stranger on earth, seeking her permanent dwelling place (Hebrews 13:14). While the church is here on earth doing the will of her Lord and preparing for her eternal home, Jesus Christ is preparing an eternal home for her. This eternal home is a holy and glorious city, built foursquare, called New Jerusalem.

Revelation 21 and 22:1-5 give a vivid description of New Jerusalem. The glory, beauty, and magnificence of the city are beyond the comprehension of the human mind. The apostle Paul wrote that such glory had never been seen, heard, or thought of in this world (I Corinthians 2:9).

We may have a partial understanding of the blessings of this eternal home when we consider the things that will pass away. There will be no death, no mourning, no curse, no tears, no pain, no sorrow, no night. These all will be gone, and in their place will be the river of life, the Tree of Life, eternal rest and joy, and eternal fellowship with Jesus Christ. Language, at its best, is inadequate to portray the realities of the life to come. One writer used the illustration of a mole burrowing in the ground and not being able to understand the life of an eagle. So it is with humans. Only when they enter through the gates of pearl will they be able to comprehend the glories of New Jerusalem.

D. APPLICATION OF TRUTH

New Jerusalem is a brand-new city that Jesus is creating for His bride, the church. Those who will have the right to enter must also new—new creatures in Christ. Heaven is a prepared place for a prepared people. Only those who are "born again" will have New Jerusalem for their eternal home.

VI. ETERNITY NEVER ENDS

A. STATEMENT OF SCRIPTURE

1. "And shall be tormented day and night for ever and ever" (Revelation 20:10).

2. "And they shall reign for ever and ever" (Revelation 22:5).

B. STATEMENT OF TRUTH

Eternity never comes to an end but continues forever.

C. EXPOSITION OF TRUTH

Just as it is foolish to try to measure space with a yard stick and a larger measurement, the light year, is necessary, so it is foolish to try to measure eternity with a measurement of time such as a year or a century. A larger measurement is necessary: an age or eon (*aion* in Greek). The New Testament uses this Greek word some 129 times, sometimes in reference to the past (Colossians 1:26) and sometimes in reference to the future (Ephesians 2:7).

This word is often pluralized, and we often have the literal expression in Greek "eon of eons." This expression may, in turn, be pluralized as "eons of eons." Such an expression occurs in Revelation 20:10 and Revelation 22:5, where it means "for ever and ever" (literally, eons of eons, or ages of ages). This term depicts ages tumbling over ages without end. They cannot be counted, for they are infinite in number. One could more readily count the sands of the sea than the ages of eternity.

We should note that this term describes the final destiny of both the wicked and the righteous.

D. APPLICATION OF TRUTH

Compared with eternity, this life is very brief. We are here only long enough to prepare for eternity. There is a heaven to gain and a hell to shun, and both are forever and ever. *Where will you spend eternity*?

QUESTIONS

1. How long is eternity?
2. Explain the meaning of the phrase "eons of eons."
3. What will be the eternal destiny of the wicked?
4. On what basis will people be judged at the Great White Throne?
5. How long is the Millennium?
6. What event will bring in the Millennium?
7. Explain the meaning of the phrase "the Tribulation."
8. Where is a safe hiding place from the coming judgments?
9. Where will Satan be during the Millennium?
10. What events will take place immediately after the Millennium?

PROJECTS

1. Write a full description of New Jerusalem.
2. Write a full description of the Battle of Armageddon.

NOTES

About the Author

RALPH V. REYNOLDS, a Pentecostal preacher for sixty-two years, has spent a great part of his life serving his church in many ways. In addition to preaching, pastoring and evangelizing, for nine years he was a member of the General Board of the United Pentecostal Church International. He also served one year on the Foreign Missions Board, three years on the Board of Christian Education, and eight years as the first resident missionary to Jamaica. While in Jamaica, Brother Reynolds started the first Bible school on a United Pentecostal mission field. He also served nine years as president of Conquerors Bible College in Portland, Oregon, and two years as the pioneer president of Apostolic Missionary Institute in Ontario, Canada. He served six years as superintendent of the old Northwest District, which then stretched from California to the North Pole and from Cheyenne, Wyoming, to the Pacific Coast. Later he was superintendent for three years of the district of British Columbia. He also served on the following district boards: Ontario District, B.C.-Washington District, Northwest District, and North Central District.

A PROLIFIC AUTHOR, his books include:

All Things to All Men
Alpha Bible Course (twenty-four units of study)
Can a Believer Be Lost?
Dear Pastor: If the Sheep Could Speak
Dividing the Word of Truth
From the Rising of the Sun
Hard Scriptures Made Easy
Home for Christmas
Living the Crucified Life
Making Full Proof of the Ministry
Milk and Honey
One Thing Thou Lackest
Portraits of the Bride
The Broken Alabaster Box
The Cry of the Unborn
The King's Highway
Truth Shall Triumph
Unbroken Vows
Upon the Potter's Wheel